Sports Junkies Rejoice!

Bill Rasmussen

Sports Junkies Rejoice!
The Birth of ESPN

Bill Rasmussen

George Conner's contributions on pages 124-125, 137-138, 172 and 214 are reprinted with his permission and gratefully acknowledged. Excerpts included in this book originally appeared in an article he authored for the University of Tulsa Annual 1981-82, pp 83, 84 and 87.

Hardcover November 1983
ISBN: 0910767017

Paperback May 2010
ISBN: 1451569572

Cover design and illustration by Wyeth Mendoza
Printed in the United States of America

Library of Congress Cataloging-in-publication data

Rasmussen, William F., 1932 -
        Sports Junkies Rejoice

More information at http://www.espnfounder.com/sportsjunkiesrejoice.htm

Preface

The story you are about to read is true. The people about whom you will read are real. They are dynamic and interesting people. Most of them, you'll like—some you won't.

There is one ground rule for reading this book. To capture the excitement of the personal emotional roller coaster I experienced in dealing with everyone who participated in the birth of ESPN, I have chosen to incorporate a "direct quote style" for many of the significant meetings and conversations. The quoted conversations are actually reconstructed from my notes, datebooks and memory and are not in any way intended to be construed as verbatim reproductions. I have been cautious in quoting others and, wherever there was a shred of doubt in my notes or recollections about the intent of any comments or thoughts of another person, they were not quoted in this manner. Obviously, direct, rather than reconstructed quotes, have all been properly credited.

Bill Rasmussen
November 30, 1983

RCA Satcom
Series Satellite

Specifications

Spacecraft Information:

Height: 37 feet with solar
    panels extended

Main Body Measurements:
    5'4" x 4'2" x 4'3"

Launch Weight: 2,378 pounds

In-Orbit Weight: 1,214 pounds

Design Life: Ten years

Orbital Elements:

Circular: Geosynchronous, 22,300
    miles above the
    equator

Period: 24 hours

Inclinations: Equatorial, zero.

Typical RCA Satcom
Series Launch

Photos and Information Courtesy RCA Americom

Opening Night
7:00 PM Eastern, September 7, 1979

This is how ESPN was introduced to the world!

Here are the first words ever spoken from ESPN's studio in Bristol, Connecticut:

"If you're a fan...if you're a fan, what you'll see in the next minutes, hours, and days to follow may convince you you've gone to sports heaven. Beyond that blue horizon is a limitless world of sports and right now, you're standing on the edge of tomorrow - sports 24 hours a day from ESPN - the Total Sports Cable Network."

Lee Leonard, ESPN

Enthusiastic Acclaim for
Bill Rasmussen, ESPN and *Sports Junkies Rejoice*

"Only Bill Rasmussen can take you back, back, back, back to the beginning of the greatest success story in the history of sports television. His ideas, his enthusiasm, his fierce determination and belief in success changed the way we all watch television and televised sports today."
Chris Berman, ESPN

"You were a man ahead of your time! A Genius - God Bless!
Dick Vitale, ESPN

What they (the Rasmussens) did was make sports and television history - nothing short of history."
John Toner, Athletic Director, University of Connecticut
Past President, NCAA

"Bill Rasmussen dramatically altered and elevated the world of sports. What he did changed the landscape of TV sports."
Sports Illustrated - Forty for the Ages
Fortieth Anniversary - 1994

"The Father of Cable Sports"
USA Today, 1994

Thanks largely to ESPN, sports in this land today are wall to wall and floor to ceiling. Just about everyone running around wearing a number has a TV camera following him or her. Total immersion is possible: When some people say today they watch "the news," they mean ESPN's SportsCenter.
The New York Times - Changing the Century

Little did he know then, but Bill Rasmussen was about to do for sports television what Thomas Edison did for electricity.
Canton (OH) Repository

Bill Rasmussen has done what every entrepreneur dreams: He found a need and filled it. Along the way, he also changed the way sports fans get their information.

Seattle Post-Intelligencer

The enthusiasm of the sports world changed the day the Whalers fired Rasmussen in 1978.

Springfield (MA) Republican

The most important day in the history of sports is August 16, 1978. That's the day Bill and Scott Rasmussen, sweltering in a traffic jam on Interstate 84 near Waterbury, Connecticut, conceived what the E. S. P. Network (later shortened to ESPN) would do with a satellite available 24 hours a day.

The Detroit News

Inspiration doesn't punch a clock. Sometimes it dawns during the depths of slumber, sometimes it rises with the steam of a shower, sometimes it is triggered by a smell or a sound. On this particular day, August 16, 1978, it is born of frustration while Bill and Scott Rasmussen sit sweltering in a Connecticut traffic jam. Traffic inches along. Heat, dust and noise unite in a sticky cacophony of misery. They don't notice. What is taking place inside their car in this hellish venue, at this unlikely time, is the creation of the basic format that one day will make ESPN recognizable around the world.

The Hartford Courant

Bill Rasmussen gave sports junkies and couch potatoes a haven in which to indulge their obsessions. His creation fed the public's growing appetite for sports. It legitimized the all-sports concept as a recipe for success in various markets and mediums, and it turned into a broadcasting giant, powerful enough to transform sports television, creatively and financially.

The Sports 100

Bill Rasmussen leaves no doubt about who are the good guys, and who are the bad. The hectic race to get ready for the first program and the countdown excitement should grip any reader.
National Book Critics Circle

They're fingerlings in a sea of oil and diversified corporate assets, but a fascinating story of father-son who plow the deep of conventional TV broadcast wisdom to spawn the idea of a 24-hour sports network
The Tulsa World

A story of some tension and drama and insight. It's a short book, told quickly and without punches pulled.
Springfield (MA) Republican

Bill Rasmussen's *Sports Junkies Rejoice* is a Horatio Alger story in space-age America. It's a fascinating diary of his journey through uncharted (television) waters.
The Hartford Courant

"Bill Rasmussen is truly the George Washington of ESPN. His accomplishments, however, transcend the boundaries of the sports arena into areas beyond our wildest dreams."
Chris Berman, ESPN

"What we're creating here is a network for sports junkies. This is not a network for the soft-core sports fans who like to watch the NFL and then switch to the news."
Scott Rasmussen
Co-founder, ESPN

UPDATE

When ESPN debuted at 7:00 PM, September 7, 1979, there were no 24 hour networks. The "Big Three" ABC, CBS, NBC did not broadcast from 1:00 - 7:00 AM. HBO was live only five hours nightly. CNN and FNC hadn't yet begun to blanket us with news 24/7. As for MTV, The Weather Channel, The Discovery Channel, The History Channel - you name it - they all came later. As a matter of fact, well over 90% of all cable systems in America had only 12 channels of programming space available in 1979 so the competition to place programming (no matter how good the provider thought it might be) was fierce.

Given that context, the idea of a total sports network operating around the clock defied imagination, yet it reached fruition in just 14 months. Naysayers abounded - especially among the broadcast giants of the day, one of whom, the President of NBC Sports, Chet Simmons, defected and signed on as President of ESPN in July 1979.

Sports fans loved the idea and soon cable companies could not even offer service unless it included ESPN. The unbelievable success enjoyed by ESPN has been chronicled thousands of times in thousands of places. Here is a "mini highlight reel" of the major facts:

- TV Households reached: US - 99,000,000
- TV Households reached: International - 300,000,000
- SportsCenter has an average 100,000,000 US viewers monthly
- TV Networks: 6 US / 46 International on all seven continents
- ESPN Radio is the largest radio network in the US and is heard on 750 affiliates

In 1979, *Sports Illustrated* opined, "ESPN may become the biggest thing in TV Sports since Monday Night Football and nighttime World Series Games." How prophetic! No one could have guessed the magnitude of the idea or the impact it would have on sports broadcasting and the way we all watch TV today. Imagine if you can, ESPN was launched before faxes, computers, the internet, email, cell phones, FedEx and UPS Overnight became part of our daily lives.

Pursuing the American Dream with tenacity, entrepreneurial daring and fierce determination, using the tools of the day, we launched ESPN. Here's to you sports junkies...Rejoice!

Bill Rasmussen
www.ESPNFounder.com
April 6, 2010

Contents

Scott Rasmussen

Ed Eagan

George Conner

Key Players

The Starting Lineup

Rasmussen, Bill....... Communications Director, New England Whalers, to President and Chairman of the Board, ESPN

Rasmussen, Scott..... Coliseum Announcer, New England Whalers, to Executive Vice President, ESPN

The Full Roster

Byers, Walter......... Executive Director, NCAA

Connal, Alan B. (Scotty) .... Executive Producer, NBC Sports, to Vice President, Broadcast Operations, ESPN

Conner, George E..... Financial Manager, Getty Oil Company Real Estate and Forest Products Division (later Diversified Operations Division)

Doherty, J.B. .... Partner, K.S. Sweet Associates

Dovey, James .... Vice President, United Cable of Plainville, Connecticut

Eagan, Edward A..... Field Agent, Aetna Insurance Co., to Vice President, ESPN; current President, Eagan Associates

Evey, Stuart W. .... Vice President, Getty Oil
                         Company Real Estate
                         and Forest Products
                         Division (later Diversi-
                         fied Operations Divi-
                         sion)

Hansen, Thomas ...... Assistant Director, NCAA

Parinello, Al. .... Manager, Satellite Sales
                         RCA Americom

Petrillo, Eugene   Senior Vice President,
    (Gene) ....   Broadcast Media,
                         D'Arcy, McManus and
                         Masius Advertising

Schneider, Gene ...... President, United Cable
                         Television, Denver,
                         Colorado

Simmons, Chester R.   President, NBC Sports, to
                         President, ESPN

Toner, John .... Athletic Director, Univer-
                         sity of Connecticut;
                         member NCAA Council;
                         former Secretary and
                         current President,
                         NCAA

Walter Byers   John Toner

1979 NCAA Television Committee

Chairman
Captain J. O. Coppedge, U.S. Naval Academy

Robert A. Seiple, Brown University
Captain J.O. Coppedge, United States Naval Academy (prior to September 1)
Maj. Gen. Raymond P. Murphy, United States Military Academy (after September 1)
Carl Maddox, Mississippi State University
Cecil N. Coleman, University of Illinois
Edwin B. Crowder, University of Colorado
Darrell K. Royal, University of Texas
George C. McCarty, University of Wyoming
Cedric W. Dempsey, University of the Pacific (prior to May 1)
Wiles Hallock, Pacific-10 Conference (after May 1)
Andrew Mooradian, University of New Hampshire
Bob Moorman, Central Intercollegiate Athletic Association
David Nelson, University of Delaware
William C. Stiles, Hobart College

Acknowledgements

Just as the efforts of countless people brought ESPN from concept to reality, so, too, did the efforts of many bring this book to completion. The encouragement, comments and contributions of family and friends is especially appreciated.

Joan Blake deserves special mention for her untold hours of feeding the manuscript to her word processor as well as her positive efforts toward correcting many of my errant thoughts.

Bill Rasmussen

Sports Junkies Rejoice!

Chapter 1

If
You
Love
Sports . . .

September 7, 1979, ESPN Plaza
Bristol, Connecticut

"If you love sports . . . if you REALLY love
sports, you'll think you've died and gone to
sports heaven. . . ." With those words, opening
night host Lee Leonard officially breathed life
into an improbable idea and made it a reality.
The idea was sports, sports and more sports, 24
hours a day, distributed nationwide via satellite
to cable television systems. With those words,
Lee Leonard opened a new era in American
telecomunications. With those words, the
Entertainment and Sports Programming
Network (ESPN) launched the purest of all
cable networks, one devoted exclusively to a narrow television target audience . . . America's
sports fans.

At precisely 7 p.m. Eastern Daylight Time,
September 7, 1979, Lee Leonard's image and

words were delivered from Bristol, Connecticut, to an RCA communications satellite, Satcom I, 22,300 miles above the equator south of Hawaii, and beamed back to earth in a fifth of a second. Sports fans everywhere had cause to rejoice. Those first words were available in less than 2 million homes nationwide, so most of the nation's sports fans weren't even aware that "sports heaven" had arrived. In September 1979, less than 16 million homes were wired for cable in this country. About 7 million of those homes received programming from the communications satellite.

As we'll see in the following pages, the launching of the Satcom I communications satellite by RCA in late 1975 changed the face of communications in the United States, particularly cable communications. Though launched in 1975, it took a while, nearly four years, before the impact of satellite-to-cable television really exploded. The technology had been perfected, but there were not enough believers to buy sufficient earth receiving stations and scatter them around the nation to make distribution via satellite viable. Many companies were experimenting with varying degrees of success with satellite distribution.

Why was ESPN different? Its arrival and announcement addressed several issues which, at the time, were not considered feasible. What company would propose programming in a single narrow area of interest, i.e., sports? Who would do a service 24 hours a day when "everyone knew" there was no television audience overnight? Perhaps the most significant question of all was, who would dare come to the cable industry with an idea that would be totally advertiser supported? Well, the "what" was ESPN and the "who" were a couple of little guys from Connecticut who knew virtually nothing of satellite technology and little more about the cable television business. However, they had a strong feeling about the sports fans of America . . . that vast army of "sports junkies"* whose insatiable appetites for sports had not been satisfied by traditional television coverage.

So there it was on September 7, 1979. The answer to a sports fan's prayer! Oh, there were a few problems, like the sound that failed to accompany the picture from the University of Colorado's football stadium in Boulder when an interview with Coach Chuck Fairbanks— ESPN's first ever remote—resulted in a beautiful picture and absolute silence. That caused a few sweaty palms in the makeshift control room in use that night; so did the fact that our next remote broadcast featured the Milwaukee Schlitz softball champions on a Budweiser-sponsored show.

---

* Phrase coined by Scott Rasmussen during a *Sports Illustrated* interview in July 1979. It has since come into common usage by the media when describing avid sports fans.

There were several far more significant questions that had to be addressed before we got to that night in Bristol, Connecticut; things like where would the money to support such a project come from? Where would the programming come from? How about the trained people to make it all work . . . where would they come from? And perhaps the biggest question of all: would the "sports junkies" of America really support a 24 hour television channel devoted exclusively to sports? That support was crucial if we expected major national advertisers to believe that this innovative, new-fangled gadget called satellite communication coupled to the cable television homes of America could really be a viable advertising medium. Any one of those questions might have caused some less ardent believers to totally abandon the project and go play golf. Not so the founders of ESPN.

Few are aware that in those anonymous days of June 1978, four people got together to discuss the crazy idea that ultimately became ESPN. One of those gentlemen, Bob Beyus, lost interest in the project within a month. Ed Eagan, now a successful consultant in the telecommunications business, saw ESPN through difficult early days that included filing for a Federal Communications Commission (FCC) license to uplink (transmit) from Bristol, Connecticut. Ed also initiated bids on studio facilities for ESPN before he left the company in January 1979. So only the author and his son, Scott, persevered through a fascinating time in their lives to stand proudly as co-founders as Lee Leonard opened an era and introduced "sports heaven" to the "sports junkies" of a sports-happy, sports-hungry nation.

And here's how it happened . . . . . .

Chapter 2

The Beginning

Saturday, May 27, 1978
Avon, Connecticut

A sparkling blue sky smiles gloriously on New England at the start of the traditional Memorial Day weekend. This weekend means summer has finally arrived, and the hardy residents of the Northeast put memories of a dreary December, January thaws, February blizzards, unpredictable March and April wind and showers behind and look to the future. For some, the future is planned no further than this weekend of anticipated fun and sun in the sand and surf at one of the many fine beaches of the area. For others, the spectacular weather generates hope that today is the day everything will go just right in the local club golf tournament. This is my group, and am I ready! The hockey season has finally ended. I'm the Communications Director of the New England Whalers of the World Hockey

Association (later to become the Hartford Whalers of the National Hockey League) —and, at least until September, no more game nights capping a 16-hour workday and no more road trips. A time to regroup, a time to enjoy the finest New England has to offer—late spring, summer and early fall, before the hockey merry-go-round starts again.

11:00 a.m

Two hours from tee time, I answer the phone without a care in the world. Well, maybe I'm thinking about keeping my drive in play on the tight first hole at the Farmington Woods Country Club in Avon, Connecticut. Other than that, as I say, not a care in the world.

"Hello"

"Hi, Bill, this is Colleen." Colleen Howe, the lady behind hockey's living legend and Hall of Famer, Gordie Howe. I had read about Gordie since my high school days in the late 1940's, and through one of those marvelous twists that life often seems to take, I had the good fortune of meeting and knowing the entire Howe hockey family—Gordie, Colleen, Mark and Marty— when Colleen negotiated a trade that brought the clan to the Whalers from the Houston Aeros in 1977. You can imagine how pleased I was when Colleen asked me to be Executive Director of Howe Enterprises in early 1978.

"What are you up to? I thought you'd be on your way to Michigan by now," I said.

"Well, I do have a flight in a little over an hour, but I had to call you," Colleen said. "This is terrible. I really didn't want to tell you this way; I'd rather tell you in person, but I don't have time and I wanted you to know as soon as possible!"

With this kind of a lead-in, I have a clue that all is not well in hockeyland.

"That doesn't sound good—what's happened?"

"Bill, we're going to terminate your relationship with Howe Enterprises. Not only that, but Howard (Howard Baldwin, Managing General Partner of the Whalers) doesn't want you back with the Whalers either. He does want you to call him Tuesday and work out your termination."

The latter was no surprise, since Howard and I have had an almost continuous running battle about a variety of things during my four years with the team.

"Well, what can I say, Colleen? I'm surprised at your comments, but obviously not Howard's."

"I'm sorry, Bill, and I don't mean to cut you short, but I do have to run and catch that plane. We'll talk when I get back. Don't forget to call Howard."

"Thanks, Colleen. See you when you get back. Have a good flight!"

Just like that, I'm unemployed. Just like that, I suddenly have a very big care in the world. Just like that, I know I won't play well in this weekend's tournament—and I don't.

Down though I feel, I know we will manage to eat and stay dry and warm and pay the bills somehow. This isn't the first time something like this has happened to me, and it probably won't be the last. What I don't know—can't possibly know—is that Colleen's call has sparked a series of events that no scriptwriter worth his salt would concoct. A series of events so loaded with emotional highs and lows, strange and incredible coincidences, and good timing that, looking back, I shudder to imagine what would have happened to me and to ESPN had Howard Baldwin not made his decision and had Colleen Howe not called. For me, the dawning of my 16th summer in New England really forced me to look to the future—and what a future it turned out to be. Here I am, 24 years out of DePauw University and about to become an "overnight success" with a national reputation in an exciting, emerging new world—the world of domestic satellite communications and cable television.

Early Days

The road of life leading to that fateful May 27th was not particularly colorful. Oh, I had done lots of interesting things, but so had millions of my peers. The only difference, perhaps, was that my early days and even my postgraduate days were always closely associated in one way or another with sports, which ultimately gave me a unique experience base from which to launch ESPN. While my contemporaries went into law, medicine or business, I spent the better part of my adult life in sports broadcasting. Just so you get to know me a little better and have a clearer understanding of events later in this book, a brief look at a bit of my history, at the people and events that helped shape my convictions about the dominance of sports in the lives of so many millions of Americans, will be helpful. You will understand why, in 1978, ESPN seemed like such a logical, albeit radical, idea for cable television and the sports junkies of America.

Born October 15, 1932, in Chicago, I grew up in Columbus Manor, Illinois, an unincorporated southside suburb of Chicago. My first memory of any significant media news coverage was December 7, 1941. We sat around that day "watching" the radio and listening to the news of the Japanese attack at Pearl Harbor. Starting in September 1946, I traveled on two buses and one streetcar each way to attend Chicago's Gage Park High School. They played real football and baseball in the city, and, by that age, I was like many 13-year-olds, totally convinced that I could play any sport.

I tried football first! My father played a long time ago in Chicago leagues when George Halas,

Red Grange and Paddy Driscoll were testing their wings in pro football's infancy, so I figured I must have some football genes in me. After all, I could catch and run—so what if I only weighed 140 pounds? I'll tell you so what! In a scrimmage one afternoon, I intercepted a pass from my defensive left halfback position (no corners, safeties, etc. in those days), moved to my right, cut left, looked upfield and saw only 60 yards of gridiron and the goalposts in front of me. Then came the moment of truth! Someone was bigger and faster than I was. As I awakened in my stretched-out position in front of the players' bench several minutes later, I decided that maybe baseball was my sport.

For the next 10 years, it was baseball—I mean baseball, baseball, baseball! There was always a game.

My glove and speed earned me an invitation to one of the Detroit Tigers Class D farm clubs for the summer of 1950 (no baseball drafts in those days) but Korea was on the horizon, and college students earned an exemption—ballplayers didn't. So it was off to DePauw University.

June, 1954

Graduation from DePauw University, Greencastle, Indiana. The Korean War (officially "police action") was in progress, and all 1954 Air Force ROTC graduates had a unique decision to make. The decision was not whether to go to work or to consider volunteering for active military duty, but rather which day we would begin active duty: July 15, September 15, November 15, or January 15! That's it! Not *if,* just *when!* My date turned out to be November 15 and, as a second lieutenant, I was assigned to Eglin Air Force Base, Florida.

The Air Force required scheduled physical fitness and recreation, and, naturally, I looked to see if my favorite sport qualified. It did, and I played third base and catcher on the HQ/AFAC team throughout my tour. (Just to put all this in proper perspective, I married Lois Ann McDonnell June 25, 1955, and we planned our honeymoon to allow for me to get back to Eglin for the annual all-star game on July 2.)

There were many others staying fit in various sports capacities at Eglin during my tour. The 1955 Eglin football team quarterback was Zeke Bratkowski of the Green Bay Packers. He threw to a couple of pretty fair wide receivers, Jim Dooley of the Chicago Bears (later Jim became head coach of the Bears) and Max McGee, later to gain Green Bay Packer, Super Bowl I, and other assorted fame as an off-field cohort of another Packer great, Paul Hornung.

November, 1956

College education and military duty completed, it was time to go to work. With only my Air Force experience and an ability to make the backhand play at third base and run, plus being a new father (Scott William Rasmussen was born at Eglin AFB March 30, 1956), I was looking for a job in the real world, not at some upcoming spring training camp as I always thought I would. However, even though I was job hunting, thoughts of sports were still very much on my mind—but now, they were thoughts of sports broadcasting. Necessity, however, put me to work at the Westinghouse Lamp Division, Bloomfield, New Jersey, in the advertising department. That was my introduction to network television, co-op advertising, point-of-purchase displays, sales material and product catalogs, etc. More importantly, I learned that a lot of money is involved in all of this. The 1957 Lamp Division budget for advertising was $3.2 million. Imagine, 3.2 million 1957 dollars just to advertise light bulbs!

May, 1959

Nearly 3½ years of experience and an MBA from Rutgers later, it was time to spread my wings in my first entrepreneurial adventure. Just two months after my second son, Glenn, was born, I left Westinghouse. I took $140 from my bank account, and, with two other young men who threw in their $140 too, we incorporated Ad Aid, Inc. and set up our advertising service business in an 800 square foot abandoned store front in East Orange, New Jersey. Nothing sports related in this move, but it was my first experience at launching a new business. I was four months short of my 27th birthday, and, as happened later with ESPN, Ad Aid, Inc. was an instant success. It virtually exploded before our eyes. To our original 800 square feet, we added another 2500 square feet in July 1959; in October, we consolidated our operations in a 15,600 square foot warehouse. By February 1960, we had added another 14,300 square feet in the same building, and our client list included Westinghouse, General Electric, General Foods, S&H Green Stamps, Congoleum Nairn and Ballantine Beer.

Anything related to sports didn't have much chance to break through my thoughts, since our business kept us working from 7 a.m. until 11 p.m. weekdays and from 8 to 5 Saturdays and Sundays. Receiving shipments, organizing individual jobs and working very hard to deliver on our promises to our customers proved to be great fun and very profitable, but actually quite boring in the execution. My restlessness pushed me to "retire" on my 30th birthday.

With a favorable settlement agreement from my two partners, I was convinced that, lack of experience notwithstanding, I would become a sports broadcaster. In October 1962 I answered employment ads in *Broadcasting,* a trade magazine, absolutely cold. One of those ads produced a trip to Westerly, Rhode Island, where a gentleman announced that he was about to start a daytime radio station in Amherst, Massachusetts, and needed a combination salesman and sports director. For the princely sum of $150 weekly, he gave me the opportunity to prepare and deliver a morning sports show at 7:45 a.m., go on the road and sell radio advertising time until 11:30 a.m., return to the studio for a 12:15 p.m. sports show, hit the road again selling for the rest of the afternoon, and return to do a late afternoon/early evening sports show. I also had to work out an agreement with the University of Massachusetts to broadcast its 1963 football schedule. How could I refuse such an opportunity?

From Westerly back to Clifton, New Jersey, to announce the decision and head for New England and quaint-quiet Amherst, home of both prestigious little Amherst College and a boisterous, building University of Massachusetts. What a change from bustling Passaic County, New Jersey, where we lived only 29 minutes from Broadway via the Lincoln Tunnel! Well, I was looking for a challenge, right? What a challenge!

I did sports broadcasts the way I imagined they should be done from what I had heard others do—it had to be that way—no experience, remember? I even got back to baseball sooner than I thought, but in a different way than I had planned—broadcasting high school baseball games in New England! Looking for experience, I found plenty. I was engineer, statistician and play-by-play man all rolled into one. And most times, the press box was nothing more than a card table and a folding chair with papers blowing everywhere.

There was some fun to be found, however, like the afternoon at Hadley, Massachusetts, when a big, left-handed hitter, whose name shall be forever lost to history, drove a long blast to deep right center field. Everyone watched as the ball bounced through a hole in the side of a shade tobacco barn, and the right fielder went in after it. Umpire's dilemma!! (This wasn't covered in the ground rules.) Should he order ground-rule double, or, depending on the potential return of the right fielder with the ball, allow what turned out to be a home run? After a debate, the home run prevailed, but it didn't really matter—the slugger's team won the game 23-1. What price experience!

September, 1963

Football play-by-play was next! Opening day for Massachusetts was at the University of Maine at Orono. I had the good fortune of spending the eight-hour drive to the edge of Maine's potato fields with the Director of Sports Information for UMass, Dick Page. Dick was scheduled to do color commentary to my play-by-play, and all the way to Maine, I debated whether to tell him that not only had I NEVER DONE a football play-by-play broadcast, I had

NEVER EVEN SEEN a major college football game. I decided it was best to say nothing and, exuding confidence, breezed through the broadcast. Surprisingly, nothing dramatic happened, and UMass won a routine game 14-0. My play-by-play career moved forward another notch.

December, 1963

Having conquered baseball and football, I figured why not try basketball? Big problem doing basketball on WTTT, Amherst. It was a daytime station, remember? I decided to go to the station manager and ask for permission to put together a small, four-station UMass night-time network for the '63-'64 UMass basketball season. Getting the stations in neighboring Northampton, Springfield, Greenfield and Pittsfield was no problem. Getting permission to broadcast games was, however. With the uttering of my first words on the network, I no longer worked for WTTT. To put it another way, I was suddenly a free-lance announcer. Not to worry! Johnny Orr was the new UMass head coach and he brought an entertaining and salable midwestern run-and-gun style to the University seldom seen in New England (Orr later recruited Doctor J—Julius Irving—for the Redmen, and still later coached Michigan to the NCAA Final Four and earned Coach of the Year honors).

Without a job, I quickly learned to sell advertising in Boston, as well as run my mini-radio network. Unknowingly, I was laying the networking, selling and organizational foundations that would be used 15 years hence.

In September 1964, I expanded the four-station UMass network from the western part of the state to an eleven-station statewide network for Redmen football, thanks to their fine season in 1963. I also progressed from selling advertising in Boston to the big boys in New York, and, with luck and a few contacts, landed S&H Green Stamps and Piel's Beer (remember Bert and Harry?) as season sponsors. The New England Plymouth Dealers and Friendly Ice Cream came on board, and I decided to expand into hockey at season's end.

December, 1964

Enter Eddie Shore, the Edmonton Express. Ask any hockey fan—even a casual one—if they've heard of Eddie Shore, and the chances are they'll say yes. He came out of the plains of western Canada in the '20's, and, long before Bobby Orr was born, brought the age of tough, rushing defensemen to the Boston Garden. Luckily for me, he lived in West Springfield, Massachusetts, and owned the Springfield Indians (later Kings, and still later Indians again) of the American Hockey League.

Eddie decided that he would allow me to do the play-by-play of some 25 games in 1964-65, but he insisted that I do them the right way, or the deal was off. The "right way" in this case was Eddie's way. For the next five seasons, I did hockey play-by-play Eddie's way—the first three, part time for him; and the next two, all games home and away for Jack Kent Cooke, owner of the parent Los Angeles Kings, who came into the National Hockey League with expansion in 1967 and acquired Springfield as a farm team. Many years earlier I had been a pretty decent skater, and when the Indians practiced at home, I was often invited to participate. For some reason, Eddie decided early on to help me skate better, then to handle a stick better, and then to shoot backhand ("Kids using curved sticks today don't understand how they're hurting their passing," he would grumble). Anyway, there I was, getting private lessons from a hockey Hall of Famer. The time on the ice actually helped my time on the air; besides, it was great fun.

January, 1965

In the midst of all this hockey experience, I had a chance to do some television. Springfield's ABC affiliate, WHYN-TV, had no sports or weather person. A part-time position was available for $10 a show, once a night, Monday through Friday. Naturally, I assumed I had been hired to do sports, right? Wrong! The general manager informed me the day before I started that he wanted me to be a weather man. Now,

the only thing I knew about the weather was
that if it was cold and snowy, it was the hockey
and basketball season; if the sun was shining and
the grass was green—let's play ball; and, if the
leaves were turning, it was football time. The
general manager won, of course, and my TV
debut was not talking about bowl games, basketball match-ups or hockey results; it was talking about low and high pressure areas and the
temperature in Burlington, Vermont; Concord,
New Hampshire; Hartford, Connecticut; and
Springfield, Massachusetts. Ingenuity rescued
me quickly, however, as I decided to include the
temperature of all American Hockey League cities in which the Springfield hockey team played,
and somehow work in the scores. Example: "Taking a look at our map tonight, it's snowing and 28
degrees in Rochester, where the Indians beat the
Americans 3-2." Or, "It's warming up in Baltimore, with spring and the playoffs just around
the corner. Outside the Civic Center, it's 40
degrees and clear tonight, and inside the Indians
whipped the Clippers 4-1 for the third straight
win." Fun, but not exactly a real television
sportscast.

May, 1965

In May 1965, WHYN-TV's competition,
WWLP-TV, the NBC affiliate in Springfield,
sent its sportscaster, Rollie Jacobs, to Raleigh,
North Carolina, as general manager of its new

television property, and needed a local replacement. Rollie, on his way to Raleigh, recommended Rasmussen and "voilá," I had my own twice-nightly sports show Monday through Friday. For the next 9½ years, I mixed WWLP-TV sports, hockey broadcasts and a variety of miscellaneous broadcasting adventures into the brewing experience pot from which ESPN ultimately evolved. What fun days I enjoyed. Long days! Interesting days! Educational days! Those were the days I met and interviewed countless numbers of great athletes: Nick Buoniconti when he was a Boston Patriot, not a Miami Dolphin linebacker; Willie Pep, one of boxing's greats (more on Willie later); Bob Cousy and Sam Jones, two of the Boston Celtics' best from their '50's-'60's glory days; Red Sox struggling newcomer Carl Yastrzemski; the incomparable Mohammed Ali when he was still Cassius Clay.

Clay trained in Chicopee, Massachusetts, for his Lewiston, Maine, bout with Sonny Liston. One afternoon, without cameras or microphones around, I talked to a very polite, articulate young man for about 40 minutes between training and public interview time, and came away with the feeling that he wasn't really positive that his mandatory poems (remember those?) for each fight and all the press hoopla were really something he wanted. Today, having nurtured his relationship with Howard Cosell, Ali might not agree with my assessments of the early Cassius Clay, but time changes us all.

My days at WWLP-TV were learning days. When I started, color TV and videotape were just arriving at local stations. So I witnessed a few "revolutionary" changes during my early days in the business. I also enjoyed the "debut" of my two sons doing television commercials for the Springfield Giants, an Eastern League baseball team. This turned out to be Scott's introduction to the business when he was all of 9 years old. We'll hear more from Scott later.

September, 1967

1967 brought new ownership to the Springfield hockey team as they became a farm club of the Los Angeles Kings. Coincidental with the new ownership, as mentioned earlier, I was hired to do play-by-play for all games, home and away. Former Detroit Redwing iron man, Johnny Wilson, was the coach, and many nights riding buses around the AHL circuit, we plotted our "major league" futures. Wishful thinking might be a better way to put it, but dream we did. "Billy, my boy," he would say, "I'm going to coach in the NHL. I'm using this job to 'stretch my knowledge' and you should, too." Johnny turned out to be quite a prophet, as he later coached both Detroit and Pittsburgh in the NHL, and Cleveland in the WHA. While he always encouraged me, neither one of us had any idea an ESPN was in the future.

To further complicate my schedule, I was also appointed a half-time instructor at Westfield State College in Westfield, Massachusetts, to work in the physical education department. This proved to be a fortunate coincidence because, during my five semesters at WSC, I gained an insight into the inner workings of men's and women's intercollegiate athletics. Paul Bogan, the athletic director, was on several national committees of the National Collegiate Athletic Association (NCAA) and the National Association of Collegiate Directors of Athletics (NACDA). His female counterpart, Marie Duffy, was the school's representative to the Association of Intercollegiate Athletics for Women (AIAW).

In 1967, the NCAA and AIAW did not cooperate in many areas. It would be the 1980's before they settled their differences. The NCAA then recognized women's sports and began to conduct both men's and women's championship events. However,countless conversations with Paul and Marie gave me my earliest education on the power of both athletics in this country and the national associations they represented. This knowledge would serve me well during the formative stages of ESPN ten years later.

April, 1974

The next building block added to my sports background was put in place in the spring of 1974. The New England Whalers, having finished their regular season hockey schedule at the Boston Garden, suddenly found they couldn't hold their playoff games there. The next best available site turned out to be the Eastern States Coliseum in West Springfield, Massachusetts, home of the American Hockey League's Kings. The significance of the switch was that I had the opportunity to meet Howard Baldwin. Not only did I meet him, but I discovered that he had no plans to cover the playoffs on radio. Naturally, I devised a plan to broadcast all playoff games, home and away, and then had to sell the idea to Baldwin.

Howard was one of the youngest owners of a professional sports franchise in America at the time and can be forgiven his somewhat inflated ego and feeling of self-importance as we met to discuss my proposal. The meeting place should have told him that the Whalers weren't quite in the major leagues yet. You see, there were no meeting facilities at the Eastern States Coliseum. The tiny press room was packed with playoff media people, so we met in—you guessed it—the men's room. Unfortunately, our relationship never really progressed from the kind of aura created by those early meetings, even

though I did go to work for the Whalers full time
in August 1974.

August, 1974-May, 1978
The Whaler years

Working for the Whalers had its rewards
(though certainly not of the financial variety!)
Traveling with a professional sports team is educational, but not necessarily as glamorous as
many people believe. There are, however, three
events worth mentioning: (1) a night of television interviews with boxers; (2) the 1977 All-
Star game in Hartford; and (3) Gordie Howe's
birthday party.

1.   During my third season with the Whalers,
Scott and I produced and aired a half-hour television show on WHCT-TV in Hartford five nights
a week, Monday through Friday. The list of
guests on that show was impressive, including
such people as Suzy Chafee, the Olympic skiier,
Janie Blalock of the LPGA, and Joan Joyce, considered by many the world's finest women's
softball pitcher. Far and away the most interesting night in "Sports Only's" history was the
night Willie Pep arranged to have a few of his
friends, who were in town for a boxing extravaganza, on our show. That night I met and
interviewed, all on one show, Rocky Graziano,
Jake LaMotta, Tippy Larkin, Paddy Demarco,
and Jersey Joe Wolcott. Boxing fans will quickly

recognize that every man was at one time in his career a world champion.

That was interesting enough, but two incidents occurred just before we went on the air that are worth telling. First, Willie brought his compatriots into the waiting room and, having lined them up, proceeded to introduce them. The last man he introduced was Jake LaMotta, and just as if it were planned in a movie, on Jake's arm was a gum-chewing, high-heeled, bleached blonde young lady. Following the introductions, Willie turned to talk about the business of the show; then, as an afterthought, he turned and looked at the blonde and said, "Oh, yeah, and that's Jake's old lady." The other incident occurred in the studio just moments before the 6:30 start of the show. With all the small talk that goes with old friends meeting and reminiscing, you can imagine the language and topics of conversation among this old friends' group reminiscences. Trying to get the group quiet so we could go on the air was problem enough, but what cracked up cameramen, directors, producers and everyone in the studio was Willie's comment that he would make sure that everyone stayed quiet until they got on camera, but in the meantime, "Don't nobody ring no bells."

The show itself turned into a shambles. Willie decided that he was going to be the master of ceremonies and interview each of his former boxing buddies. While fighters may be able to tell within a second how long three minutes is in the ring, put a microphone in their hand, and they're at a total loss. It was a fun and interesting night, and of all the boxers I met that night, Jersey Joe Wolcott came off as the consummate gentleman.

2.   Howard Baldwin gave me the task of producing the 1977 WHA All-Star game, and "what a show we gave 'em," as the saying goes. The event stands out in my memory because, in addition to my doing the national play-by-play broadcast on PBS, Scott handled the ceremonies, introductions, etc. on the ice before a jam-packed Civic Center crowd. It was our "national debut," if you will, that would be repeated with ESPN less than two years later.

3.   Just a year after the All-Star game, a near disaster struck the Hartford Civic Center. Straining under tons of snow, the arena roof collapsed just hours after a basketball crowd had left. Fortunately, not one person was injured, but suddenly the Whalers were without a home. Arrangements were hastily made to play the remaining games of the 1977-78 season at the Springfield Civic Center, 25 miles north of Hartford.

The roof collapse was the reason Gordie Howe's birthday party was held in Springfield on March 29, 1978. This was an extravaganza rivaling the All-Star game, but there was only one star, 50-year-old Gordie Howe. Lots of celebrities

were on hand from Gordie's past, including Ted
Lindsay, Al Kaline, Tony Trabert, Eddie Shore
and more. The mandatory 800-pound cake was
skated to center ice by some peewee hockey
players, and the full house never sounded hap-
pier than when everyone joined in singing
"Happy Birthday." I was more than a little
happy myself since this was another opportunity
for Scott and me to combine talents. We wrote
and published the printed souvenir program for
the evening, and wrote the script used in the on-
ice ceremonies. Of course, Scott did the in-house
announcing while I was the stage manager and
overall director of the event. This proved to be
the last of the pre-ESPN building blocks to be
put in place.

Colleen's phone call came less than two
months later.

Chapter 3

First Steps

Tuesday, May 30, 1978
Hartford, Connecticut

With the golf tournament and phone call behind me, I figure I might as well call Howard and discuss my termination as Colleen suggested.

"Good morning. New England Whalers."

"Good morning, Bill Rasmussen calling for Howard Baldwin."

"One moment, please."

"Bill." Howard didn't sound happy.

"Yes, Howard, Colleen asked me to call you to talk about my termination."

"Well, we're finished—through. I'll pay you until the end of June, and that's it." Reconciliation was obviously not on Howard's mind.

"Should I plan to come in and see you today or tomorrow?" I asked.

"What for? If you don't like what I just told you, I'll stop your pay at the end of the week. There's nothing to talk about, and you don't have to come in and see me."

"O.K. I'll just come in and clean out my desk."

"Good! We'll mail your last check through the 30th. Thanks for calling."

And that was that.

In spite of my stormy four years with the Whalers, I must say there were some pluses associated with the job. The biggest one by far was my introduction to the budding cable television industry in Connecticut.

Connecticut was one of the last states in the country to allow cable television. It was 1972 before any company was allowed to begin cabling its franchise area. A year after I joined the Whalers in 1974, the biggest system in the state, United Cable of Plainville, still had only 9500 subscribers. One of my first tasks with the Whalers was to try to arrange some local TV coverage. Since the local broadcast properties were not at all interested in providing coverage, I turned to cable.

Before I go any further, I'd better tell you that my knowledge of cable at this point was meager. I soon discovered the cable industry was born in the hills of Pennsylvania in the early 1950's. An enterprising gentleman discovered that TV reception was poor because of all the hills. He decided to put up a higher antenna and literally "connect" his friends by wire (cable) to his antenna. He split the cost with his neighbors (subscribers), and the cable industry was conceived.

For approximately 25 years, the cable industry was an extension of that enterprising Pennsylvanian. The industry believed its mission was to provide better television reception in areas (always outside metropolitan complexes) that had inferior quality TV.

In December 1975, RCA Americom launched a domestic communications satellite from the Kennedy Space Center in Florida that changed the cable business forever. During its first quarter-century, the industry had been a hardware-oriented as opposed to a programming-oriented business. Each system was concerned only about delivering as many quality TV signals to as many subscribers as possible. Operators had almost no concern for programming, and programmers had the same kind of non-interest in the cable industry because the number of homes served was so small compared to the potential audience of the big three national networks, ABC, CBS and NBC. As you will note on the following chart, only in the last five years has the cable industry expanded significantly in numbers of subscribers. The reason is really very simple. The technology and the programming were successfully wed, and cable television came out of the dark ages of hardware—only to

become an industry providing an alternative programming option to millions of Americans dis-
gusted or disgruntled with the national network
fare:

	Number of Cable Households in US	% of Cable to Total TV Households
1976	12,094,000	17%
1977	13,194,000	18%
1978	14,155,000	19%
1979	16,023,000	21%
1980	18,672,000	24%
1981	22,596,000	28%
1982	27,500,000	32%
1983	30,636,000	37%

Source: *Cablevision* Magazine—Figures as of Oct.
1982

It was the happy marriage of cable technology
and programming that made ESPN possible, but
I'm getting ahead of myself. Let's finish the
cable discussion before getting back to the story.

RCA wasn't exactly flooded with orders for its
new satellite in 1975, and the reason was under-
standable. The satellite in the sky worked fine,
but there were only two receiving stations on
earth, one in Jackson, Mississippi, and the other
in Fort Pierce, Florida.   .

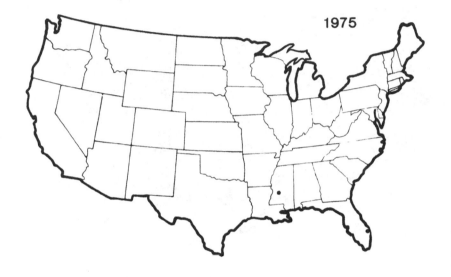

1975

Illustration courtesy of RCA Americom.

In late 1978 there were less than 300 earth
stations located at cable systems around the
country. That number had grown to just under
3,000 by 1980.

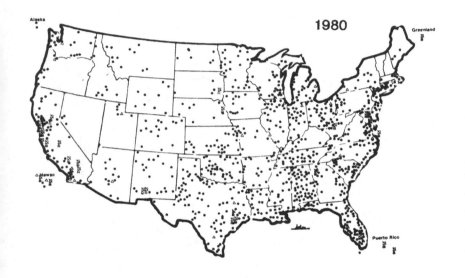

Illustration courtesy of RCA Americom.

Today there are well over 20,000 earth stations
sprinkled around America.

Take a brief look at the following illustration
to understand how very simple domestic satellite
transmission is. The transmitting station
(uplink) on earth beams a signal to the satellite
22,300 miles above the equator, which then
retransmits the signal in a wide pattern (foot-

print) that can be received by earth stations anywhere within its coverage area.

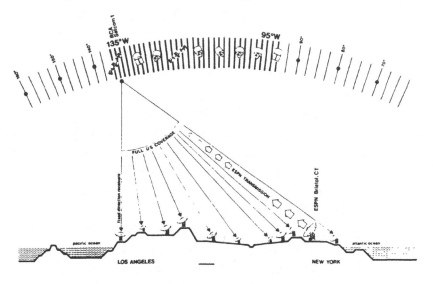

Illustration courtesy of RCA Americom.

Now you may ask, what is so special about the satellite? From a quality of signal point of view, it is far superior to a standard broadcast signal. More significant, however, is the economic bene-fit. Traditional terrestrial broadcasters must have their broadcast signals re-amplified and retransmitted constantly across the country. Obviously, this is an expensive proposition and, in fact, broadcasters are charged by the mile depending on how far they have that signal retransmitted. In other words, it costs approximately ten times as much to deliver a television signal 1,000 miles as opposed to 100 miles.

The advantage of the satellite is that, once you have paid for your lease of a channel (transponder), you may deliver programming to that channel and have it retransmitted to 1, 100, 1,000 or 10,000 earth receiving stations at no additional charge. The economics are obvious. A simple experiment quickly demonstrates how a satellite can deliver a signal simultaneously to all points of the United States. Take a flashlight and hold it one foot above the book you're now reading. The circle of light is very small. Now move that flashlight up two more feet, and the circle of light increases. Now let your imagination do the rest of the work. Assume that the satellite is a giant flashlight in the sky, retransmitting television signals. Imagine taking the flashlight in your hand and moving out to a point in space 22,300 miles above the earth. The beam of that flashlight would splash a pattern of light across North America roughly equivalent to the footprint of Satcom I, illustrated below:

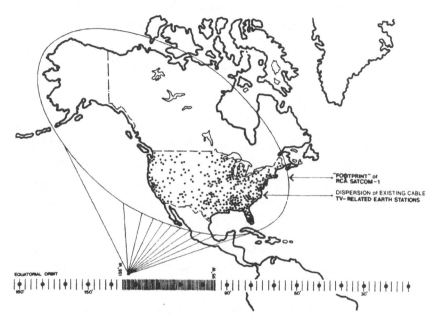

EQUATORIAL ORBIT

Illustration courtesy of RCA Americom.

Time to get back to June 1978 and our tentative first steps.

Monday, June 5
Plainville, Connecticut

Enter Ed Eagan. I had met Ed while wandering the halls of the Hartford Civic Center in 1975. He worked for an Aetna insurance agency located on the same floor as the Whalers' administrative offices. Ed was unaware of my Whalers' termination when he called me Thursday, June 1, to ask me to be a guest on a new series of TV shows he was preparing for cable distribution. Until the phone call, I had had no idea he had any interest in television, but he had a partner, Bob Beyus, with some television remote equipment and seemed excited about the prospects for his new show. Obviously, I told him I no longer worked for the Whalers and probably wouldn't qualify as a guest on his proposed show. But I said that I'd like to meet with him and discuss a variety of ideas that had been rolling around in my head about television production and sports television in New England.

Beyus was actually our host since he had a contract for services with United Cable of Plainville, and part of his payment was the use of the tiny 10′ by 12′ office in which our meeting was held.

"Hi, Bill, Scott—glad you could make it—say hello to Bob Beyus," Eagan greeted us. Earlier I had related my conversation with Ed to my son, Scott, and, with his Whaler background, he thought the prospects of something interesting coming out of the meeting were pretty good, so he came along.

Eagan continued, "Bob is the owner of Live Video and has been working with me shooting our pilot show—it's on hot air balloons."

You may think I'm kidding, but spring and early summer bring out plenty of hot-air balloons in the Farmington River Valley of Connecticut, and, as I was to discover later in the day, Ed and Bob really did have some hot-air balloon footage.

"We think we can do a half-hour show each week, and bicycle it to the state cable operators," Ed said.

Beyus added, "The nice thing is that it won't cost very much up front, because whatever equipment I don't have in my truck or studio, I can make arrangements to use here."

"You mentioned some ideas you had when I called last week, Bill. What did you have in mind?" asked Ed.

"Since the Whalers moved to the Civic Center," I said, "we've been trying to get some games televised. Have you talked to any of the systems about live sports?"

"Too expensive," Bob objected. "No system can afford the production! We have tried some baseball with the Bristol Red Sox. With a down-and-dirty, two-camera shoot, we can do games. The quality's not the greatest, but cable people don't demand broadcast quality."

Bob's comment left me with an early perception that really registered, i.e., cable people in 1978 felt inferior to the networks. They didn't feel they had to match "network quality." That perception would prove a reality in the months ahead. Programming simply was not a local cable system concern.

"How about basketball?" I asked, "or any other sports, for that matter? Have you talked to any of the colleges in Connecticut?"

Eagan answered, "No, but we could. Maybe we could mix their programming with ours and use highlights or something."

By now Scott couldn't contain himself. "What's wrong with doing live play-by-play?" he asked.

What's wrong indeed???!!

A long discussion ensued. That discussion centered generally around the technical capabilities of Live Video and the potential interest of the cable systems in Connecticut. Scott and I wanted to get to the programming business quickly, but Bob and, to a lesser degree, Ed posed some very significant roadblocks.

There was no question lots of mental wheels were spinning in that room, and we all sensed that we were on to something that could prove very exciting. We had a spark of an idea—just a spark!

"I'll talk to a couple of the colleges," I said.

"Leave the Whalers to me," Scott added. "You might not work with them any more, but I still do, and we all know they really need TV help."

Bob, with his by-now familiar unemotional style, said, "I'll see if I can talk to Jim (Jim Dovey, vice president of United Cable of Plainville) about the idea, but doubt if he'll be interested."

"This will take a lot more money than we've been thinking of," said Ed, "but let me work on it and we'll get together again on the weekend."

Summarizing our day was easy:

1. We didn't know much about the cable systems and their working relationships.

2. We had no idea if the teams would be interested.

3. We didn't know if any viewers really cared about a steady diet of Connecticut sports and would watch even if we solved items 1 and 2.

So there we were at the end of the day—super idea! Wow! Great! What do we do next? Schedule another meeting, that's what!

Saturday, June 10
Plainville, Connecticut

Back in Bob's tiny office, we compared notes on our week's activities.

I started. "I met with Don Russell, the Athletic Director at Wesleyan, and he's interested but really thinks his school is a little small. John Toner, at UConn (University of Connecticut) wants to pursue the idea a little further and thinks maybe his alumni can help since so many stay in the state after graduation. I said I'd get back to him when I had a little more information about the cable people."

"The Whalers are interested," Scott injected, "but don't really believe anything will come of our idea. They basically said they'll wait and see."

Bob Beyus was next. "Jim Dovey thinks there will be interest among the Connecticut cable operators, but doesn't think we have done enough homework to understand what we're talking about."

"On the money side," Eagan offered, "I think I can put together a $300,000 package with individual units at $5000 each. It will take some time, but by August, we ought to have some money."

Summarizing: we had aroused a little curiosity in a few people who basically said, "Great, but we don't think you can pull it off," and we didn't have any solid prospects for financing our project.

We decided during this meeting to gain as much knowledge as possible in the next two weeks and scheduled a meeting in the United Cable conference room for Monday, June 26. The invited guests were the Connecticut cable operators, and our thought was to unveil our Connecticut sports package to them and hear firsthand their collective reaction.

Saturday, June 17
Avon, Connecticut

Scott invited Ed and me to his condo to come up with a company name. We wanted the words "sports" and "network" in the name. Since Connecticut sports events were not played every day of the year, we had to address another potential use of the air time for our proposed Connecticut system. HBO and Showtime were taking care of the movie fare for the cable industry at that point in history, and, besides, "The Movie and Sports Channel" didn't have a good ring to it. Any other kinds of programs that we could come up with all had something lacking, until finally we hit on just the general word "entertainment." Entertainment and sports aren't really very specific. Scott recalls how we finally settled on the name.

"My father always liked hokey things, and he liked the double meaning of the letters ESP. It was the corny kind of thing that he used to do on his television show and had done with the Whalers, but it always seemed to work. Besides, Ed and I couldn't come up with anything better.

"Seriously, we did kind of like the way the network initials looked, and we agreed that, no matter what we did in the future, it certainly would fall under the entertainment and sports umbrella, so we had our new network name—the E.S.P. Network."

Monday, June 26
Plainville, Connecticut

Only about half of the state's cable companies were represented at the meeting. Jim Dovey, our "landlord" (he volunteered the use of his conference room), had prevailed upon some of his fellow cable executives to hear our idea, or we might have had even fewer.

"Good morning, I'm Bill Rasmussen. We're delighted you were able to arrange your schedules to be here, and we think we have something interesting to tell you. First, let me introduce Ed Eagan, Scott Rasmussen and Bob Beyus. The four of us have spent a lot of time this month talking and brainstorming an idea that seems to be made for cable TV. Our idea is to package Connecticut college and university sports, mix in the New England Whalers, and provide the service to you via an interstate network."

"Before you go any further, do you realize how expensive this is?" asked Paul Hancock, broadcasting veteran and owner of New Milford Cable.

"Well, it doesn't have to be expensive—if we bring the service to a common point and feed you folks," I answered.

"We don't have a common point for all our programming," said Jeff Reynolds of Valley Cable in Seymour, Connecticut. "We all belong to different MSOs (Multiple System Operators) or are independent. We each arrange for our own programming."

Ed Eagan asked, "What about HBO—you all carry that?"

Jim Dovey answered, "Yes, Ed, we do, but some of us receive it via Eastern Microwave, and some relay it to each other."

It was obvious we were not instantly accepted as the purveyors of an immediate hit that the operators simply couldn't do without.

"Have you thought about the satellite?" someone asked.

Thought about it? We didn't even know about it! If the truth were known, we came into this meeting with two weeks of enthusiasm, a concept, open minds and little else in the way of operational knowledge of the cable industry.

"No, not really," I said. "What about it—what do you think?"

"You really ought to investigate the possibilities," Jim Dovey suggested. "I'm sure RCA would be happy to talk to you."

Scott asked, "What does it do, and how much does it cost?"

That did it! Throughout the meeting there had been a sense of growing excitement and enthusiasm on both sides, and Scott's question seemingly triggered everyone's tongue at the same time.

"It covers the eastern 18 states."

"You can reach all of New England with it."

"It's only $100 an hour for some things."

"No, it's $4000 an hour, but you need to get the signal to New Jersey for that price."

And on and on. We learned more in a few minutes at this meeting than we had since Ed first called me three weeks previously. The bottom line was that the operators didn't really understand all the specifics of the satellite, but their message was loud and clear:

"In a matter of months we'll all be receiving satellite signals, and no matter what it takes, if you want to get programming to us, it had better come from the satellite."

From the back of the room, "How are you going to produce all these games? It takes money and equipment to do that."

Anticipating just this question, I had arranged with a friend who owned Telfax Productions to detour one of his broadcast remote trucks through Plainville on a trip from Boston to Rochester. This allowed me to say, "We intend to use broadcast quality units to produce these events, not two camera, ¾ inch sub-broadcast quality equipment. We believe that to be successful we have to satisfy your viewers, and they will demand quality—the same quality they get from the networks. To show you what we plan to use, a Telfax van is parked out front, and as soon as we finish here, I'd like all of you to take a moment and walk through it."

Paul Hancock again, "Why do you want to spend all that money? We do things with two cameras in black-and-white. If people want to watch, they don't care about fancy trucks."

"Our point exactly," I answered. "We think they do care, and, to be successful, we'll have to compete on the broadcast level, not the cable level represented by two-camera, black-and-white units."

After some more small talk and a rehash, the meeting kind of disintegrated into small pockets of conversation and some tours of that Telfax van.

Undaunted by the few cautioning responses we received at our meeting with the cable operators, we set about the business of putting a proposal together for the programming. How to acquire it—how to produce it—how to charge the subscribers, etc. Throughout the week, we tried a variety of ideas and finally settled on a plan.

Thursday, June 29

"John, (John Toner, A.D. at UConn) Bill Rasmussen calling about that cable idea we discussed a couple of weeks ago."

"Yes, Bill, how's it going?"

"Well, I'd like to get your reaction to a proposal we've come up with to put about 25 to 30 UConn events on the air next year."

"Fine! I'm going out of town tomorrow and won't be back 'til the 10th." (I soon learned that John was on the road frequently because of his NCAA involvement. He was a member of the NCAA council [sort of the Board of Directors of the NCAA] and a very powerful voice that would be heard on our behalf in later dealings with the NCAA.) "How about lunch at the Faculty Center, and we'll see what you have."

"Sounds good! See you then."

Well!! Now we had survived a meeting with the cable operators and had an invitation from one potential program service to talk further! We were on our way. Time to tell the world!

As a general rule, I have discovered during my lifetime there are two approaches available for use when you have something to say:

1. Be cautious, tentative and don't rock the boat—someone may laugh at you; or

2. exude confidence, be positive, believe that what you're saying will be done, and, when people laugh at you, maintain your confidence. Those people will soon discover that you were right.

I don't have to tell you which path we chose. As we gathered in Bob's office at United Cable, I was already mentally writing a news release and visualizing the media list we were going to invite to a press conference we were about to schedule.

"Brace yourselves, guys," Scott said as we got down to business, "my father has something to tell you."

"Bob, Ed—we all know this idea will work. Somebody will do it—it might as well be us. One way to establish ourselves is to tell the world what we have in store for it. I'm talking about a press conference, interviews—the works! In the meantime, I'll write a press release and get it printed."

About 10 seconds of silence followed. Then came the reaction:

"Great, this is great—we're on our way," Eagan enthused.

"Now, wait a minute," said Beyus. "We can't just call a press conference and . . ."

"Why not?" I asked.

"Well, because we don't know enough about the cable business, and we don't have any contracts for programming, and, even if we did, we don't have any customers."

"We will, though," Ed offered. "We can sell UConn sports fans a package for the season, and Bill and I are meeting with Toner next week."

"I still don't like it," Bob noted. "But O.K."

It's fair to say that Bob was probably right, but, from the beginning, it was understood that we each owned 25% of whatever it was we were putting together and, in reality, he was outvoted.

"How about our space?" Scott asked. Following our cable meeting we had asked Jim Dovey to rent us some additional space. He had an empty room approximately 20'x20' that we sought for some desk space for Ed, Scott and myself.

Ed and Bob had been working on this, and, much to our delight, Ed reported, "We can move in Saturday."

Scott, "What are we going to move in? We don't have any furniture."

Ed was ready for that one. "My apartment has just been redone, and all the closet doors replaced. We can get some legs from a lumber yard and put them on the four corners of the doors that were taken down and have three desks." (It sounded easy enough, and we did get the doors and legs Saturday, but, not being a handyman, I forgot the brackets so we couldn't build our "desks" until Monday.)

Beyus spoke up. "I'm not sure I like the way this is heading. Maybe you guys would be interested in buying my equipment, and I'll just be a technical service or subcontractor. I'm not sure I want to own part of this."

Enter the pessimist! Obviously, Bob was not too comfortable with our direction. We talked a long while and didn't resolve anything concerning his role, but we did schedule that press conference.

Friday, July 7
Plainville, Connecticut

Written and telephoned invitations had gone out to about 35 area media people for our press conference. Bob, Ed, Scott and I were at the head of the same United Cable conference table that had been surrounded by cable operators less than two weeks ago.

Given my past working relationships with the various members of the area media, I expected that, out of courtesy, if not curiosity, at least half of the 35 invitees would be on hand. I was more than a little unhappy with the turnout as I greeted three reporters; a fourth showed up late. In spite of the small turnout, I charged ahead with a quick opening summary and then introduced Ed, Bob and Scott.

Blank stares were my reward for those opening remarks. "We plan to launch a cable pay service to deliver UConn sports to all the cable systems in Connecticut. Our first event will be the UConn-Navy game Saturday, September 16th at Storrs. We'll also do soccer and follow up with basketball, hockey and baseball as well as other events. We plan to sell the package with the help of UConn at a price of $18.00 per subscriber for all events televised during the school year."

Skeptical stares were my reward for these comments.

Eagan jumped in, "Cable systems need to have additional programming, and what better way to start than with UConn sports? We will also add other events and expand to other states in New England in the future." (Ed was right in the optimist mode.)

WTIC radio announcer Lou Palmer pointed out, "You can't televise NCAA football on Saturdays."

"That's generally true," I said, "but there are exceptions granted. We are investigating that right now."

The *Journal Inquirer's* Matt Buchler asked, "How many customers do you have for this?"

Oh-oh! Now we're on thin ice. "We're planning a mailing to UConn alumni in the future, and today's press conference is the first public announcement, so at the moment, Matt, we have no customers.

We literally meandered through a lot of questions—all loaded with doubt and skepticism—and wrapped up our brief, brief press conference with:

"We'll have much more information shortly along with a schedule and get back to you."

Very definitely a modest beginning for the E.S.P. Network!

During our post-mortem of the press conference, Bob Beyus said, "Guys, I have to talk to you. I don't operate this way, and I'm getting out. I'll be happy to rent you equipment if I can help, but I don't want any part of this—you're crazy!"

With that proclamation, Bob left. Ed, Scott and I were each suddenly 33⅓ owners of our idea.

Ed and I met with John Toner on Monday, July 10, and moved our discussions along. Later the same day, we met Scott to assess our progress.

"We've got to formalize our company," Scott suggested.

"You're right!" Ed agreed. "Do you guys have an attorney you prefer to use? If not, I've been working with Bob Hempstead in Hartford."

"Get him on the phone!"

Ed called Hempstead, and we set a meeting for Friday, July 14, 1978, to discuss incorporation.

Chapter 4

Concepts, Satellites and Transponders

Friday, July 14, 1978
Hartford, Connecticut

Incorporating a company is amazingly easy. An attorney draws up some papers; you devise a very broad purpose, write a check for the registration with the state and away you go.

Incorporating E.S.P. Network was just that simple. Scott, Ed and I are the three incorporators of the company, and, as originally formed, the President was Ed while Scott and I were VP's. (Ed won the top billing since his attorney drew the papers.) Scott paid the $91.00 Connecticut State registration fee, and we were incorporated on July 14, 1978.

Later that same day we held our first business meeting.

"Now that we're incorporated, we'll have to get State and Federal tax numbers and some real stationery; but first, we really need some money," Ed said. You'll recall that I hadn't collected any pay since June 30. Scott only collected a regular pay during the hockey season, and Ed was an insurance agent working on a sports project, which didn't enhance his commissions.

"I've got some credit cards," I joked. "We can get some money there!"

Ed volunteered, "I can't help much from the personal side, but I've got a few people interested in our $5000 packages."

"The $91.00 cleaned me out, so don't look at me," said Scott. Then, looking at me, he added, "Let's get back to your credit cards, though. How much can you raise?"

"I'll have to check, but I suppose seven or eight thousand dollars." (It proved to be $9,000). "Tell you what—whatever I can raise, we will divide by three, and that will be our start-up investment. You two can borrow the money and pay me back when we get an investor or however we raise funds," I suggested.

We quickly agreed, and then graciously granted ourselves $2,000 monthly salaries. Expenses were limited to rent and phone, and, with luck, we now had until September 1 to find some more money.

I should tell you that we were now "comfortably settled" in our "closet-door-desk" one-room office, complete with telephones. We wired our phone system to the United Cable receptionist's desk so she could answer for us and make it sound a little professional. To add to the aura of being a going business, whenever we went to lunch, we put our phones on "hold" to give callers a busy signal and not let them know just how thin our organization really was.

One suggestion from our printer, Guy Wilson, owner of Lithographics, Inc., provided all three of us with four different business cards. On our cards, we were all VP's and, depending on the particular discussion or meeting, we were either VP Marketing, Programming, Finance, or blank (to meet any situation not covered by the first three.) Fortunately, all of that was short lived.

Thursday, July 20
Plainville, Connecticut

As a result of our June meeting with the cable operators, Al Parinello, RCA's marketing man, scheduled a meeting with us in Plainville. In anticipation of his arrival, we again turned to Jim Dovey, now our legitimate landlord, and arranged to rent his conference room for the afternoon. The fee: $20.00. (We had to do this because we didn't want a representative of a major company seeing our very low-budget offices.)

After the amenities, Parinello began his education of both Scott and me:

"How much do you know about Satcom I?"

"Very little," we admitted. "We don't even know the area you cover with it."

"That's a simple one—the whole country," he answered. "We have an uplink facility in Vernon Valley, New Jersey, and, depending on what you have in mind, we can uplink your signal from there."

"We're planning to originate our programming from here," Scott commented. "Do we have to be uplinked from New Jersey, or is that just an option?"

"Only an option," Al said, "but you know it will be *very*, *VERY* expensive to build your own uplink."

"Let's not worry about that just yet. Tell us about your charges for transponder time." I wanted to hear the details first, then worry about the operational problems.

For the next 45 minutes, Al related all of the various time usage and price quotes available on his rate card. The card itself is too detailed to reprint here, but let me just note that in 1978 RCA was selling anywhere from one occasional hour to five hours nightly. Prior to the meeting, we had no idea of what to expect. Following Al's explanation, we felt we could afford $1250 a night for five hours seven days a week even though we still had no money.

"You'll have to excuse me," Scott said, "I'm sorry I can't stay, Al, but I have an appointment."

"We're about finished anyway," Al said, "I'll tell your father anything else there is to know. Good to meet you, Scott." With that, Scott left.

"Looks like we'll want to talk to you about five hours a night, Al," I summarized. "We'll want to talk about it, of course, but we'll let you know as soon as possible."

Al didn't look like he was ready to leave, and he wasn't.

"There is one other rate that's not on the card. I suppose I should mention it. You can take a pre-emptible transponder with an escalating payment plan for about $35,000 monthly. It's a five year lease, however, and there is a termination liability."

"O.K.—anything else?" I was really planning on the five hours a night and just made notes as he explained the pre-emptible.

"Nope, that's it! Call me when you determine what you want. Thanks for your time—it sounds like you're on to something good."

Later that night Scott stopped in to hear what he had missed, if anything.

"Not much, really, just one other rate that wasn't on the card. It's a 24-hour daily rate, though, not something we'd want."

Curiosity prompted Scott to ask, "How much is a 24-hour transponder?"

"About $35,000 a month for the first year, and then it goes up."

Scott let his mental computer work a bit, and then his eyes lit up. "That's less money than for five hours! Are you sure $35,000 is the right number?"

"Look at these notes," I answered a bit irritably.

"Pre-emptible 24-hour transponder, $35,000 monthly, with an increase after 12 months. What do you mean, less than five hours—that's impossible!"

"That's why I asked if $35,000 is the right number! Dad, at that rate we can buy a 24-hour transponder for about $1143 a day instead of five hours a night for $1250. How many of these transponders does he have for sale?"

"I didn't even ask him," I confessed. "I was just being courteous and took down the notes, but I was really planning on the five hours a night."

Scott was really excited now. "When will you talk to him again? We should order three transponders, if he has them"

From Al's conversation earlier in the day, I guessed that three transponders would be available, but I cooled Scott's enthusiasm. "We don't even know what we'll do with one, much less three, and where would we get the money?"

We argued transponders—three, two or one— well into the early morning hours and agreed to call to order one the next day, but to keep alert for additional uses and the possible demand for additional transponders.

Friday morning I called Al and said, simply, "We'll take one!"

"One what?" he asked.

"One of your 24-hour transponders."

Absolute silence! Finally, "You will? Great!"

"Just tell us what we have to do and how soon we'll owe you some money."

"You'll have to send me a letter confirming this phone call, but there's no real rush. Wait until I check other requests because you'll have to start your monthly payments 90 days after we award you the transponder," Parinello informed me.

"Now that we've decided, we don't want to lose it," I said.

"Don't worry, if activity picks up and it looks like we have some other firm orders, I'll let you know and you can get that letter to me," Al concluded.

"Fine, we'll stay in touch." I hung up. Scott and Ed were grinning; so was I. We had just ordered a transponder and had no idea of how to pay for it or how to acquire 24 hours of programming for it, but unofficially, we had it. No money down and even 90 days after official announcement before the first payment was due.* Not

---

* This was the last transponder awarded by RCA under these terms. When additional transponders were awarded later in 1978, monthly payments started immediately.

(footnote continued on next page)

bad, considering a similar transponder's rights were sold for $5 million two years later and resold within the following year for $10.4 million.

"Now we can really get to work with UConn," Ed suggested. "And I know someone at Lipman AMC Motors who can get us involved with the AMC race people for some regional races here in New England."

Scott was mulling something in his mind. Later that day, Ed and I saw the results of that

---

(footnote continued from preceding page)

While the monthly tariff rates remained rigidly controlled, the value of transponder space escalated rapidly. In November 1980, the Getty Oil Company purchased the right to use transponder 21 on Satcom I from Satellite Syndicated Systems, Tulsa, Oklahoma, for $5 million. Getty's intended use for that transponder never materialized and just over six months later it sold its rights for $10.4 million to Landmark Communications, Norfolk, Virginia. Later in 1981 RCA held an auction for transpon ders on Satcom IV, a much less desirable satellite than Satcom I (later replaced by Satcom 3R), and the ultimate price per transponder was $13.4 million. In 1982, industry experts estimate the value of rights to a transponder on Satcom 3R, the primary cable television satellite, at $20 million each. These are the same rights we acquired in 1978 for $0. Had we pursued Scott's initial suggestion of acquiring three transponders instead of the one we did acquire, and had RCA approved our application, ESPN today would be utilizing three transponders on the primary cable bird worth approximately $60 million. In 1978 we didn't know any better, and we were happy with our one transponder.

mulling. In a memo that he had pecked out on our borrowed typewriter, Scott said, "We should plan a full national service. The UConn $18.00 plan will not fully utilize the transponder and will probably not generate enough cash to justify starting the project."

Skepticism was voiced by both Ed and me, but Scott made a very logical argument centered around full utilization of the facility we had just acquired from RCA.

Slowly, he began to convince us that he was right.

The next few weeks were spent working with John Toner at UConn on our Connecticut package and debating our national vs. regional approach. Scott adamantly advocated full national service, while Ed pushed for the regional approach. As for me, I questioned Scott about what we could do for 24 hours a day (that was one he couldn't answer) and worked with Ed on the UConn project, all the while wondering which approach was right.

Wednesday, August 16
Waterbury, Connecticut

The national vs. regional impasse was broken on my daughter Lynn's 16th birthday. She was at the beach in New Jersey, and Scott and I planned to leave early and drive four hours to spend the day helping her celebrate.

Less than 30 minutes into the trip, we were backed up in a massive traffic jam on Interstate 84 in Waterbury, Connecticut. August in Connecticut is typically hot and humid, and today was typical. Stuck in traffic, with both the temperature and humidity approaching 90 and riding in an air-conditionless Mazda GLC, it didn't take long for tempers to fray. We were still trying to figure out what to put on that transponder when Scott said, "Play football all day, for all I care."

To this minute, I don't know if that was just a random, intuition-inspired statement or something he had had in his mind for a while.

After a slight hesitation, while some mind-mulling of my own happened, I said, "Why not?"

"What do you mean, 'why not'?"

I continued, "The NCAA plays hundreds of football games every Saturday, and ABC only televises a few of them. Why can't we do four or five of the leftovers?"

Now Scott warmed to the subject. "They can't be live! I don't know the NCAA rules, but I know they can't be live."

"You're right, they can't. At least, not now, but maybe we can convince them to change the rules."

"I doubt it," Scott grumbled.

Suddenly, waiting for the traffic jam to dissolve didn't seem so annoying. Scott continued,

"Who do we know at the NCAA—how do we pursue this?"

"We can figure that out later. Let's talk about what else we can do. The NCAA plays lots of other sports, too."

"Yeah, basketball, soccer, baseball—hey, maybe we can fill our transponder with live events and replays at odd hours," Scott offered.

"And another thing," I said, "we can do a half-hour show nightly and updates between events—nothing but sports, sports and more sports."

The traffic jam melted away at just about the same time our transponder dilemma did, and we were sailing along toward New Jersey totally caught up in our idea.

"Let's start making notes," Scott said, and pulled out his ever-present yellow legal pad. "We have to talk about remote trucks . . ."

"Build 'em or rent them?" I interrupted.

"Build our own, of course," he answered. "And we'll need studios, and we should uplink our own signal . . ."

I interrupted again, "We'll need plenty of talent (announcers), and we ought to have a big name or two . . ."

"I vote for Phyllis George," Scott broke in.

"We can hire remote production crews, but we'll need bodies in the studio to tie it all together," I continued.

"Where can we build a station?" Scott asked. "We'll get Ed's thoughts on that tomorrow."

We were in New Jersey at the birthday party before we knew it, and I guess Scott and I owe Lynn an apology for that day—we weren't very interested party-goers.

The ride back to Connecticut was filled with more of the same frantic suggestion-question-answer-planning in which we had been engaged on the way to New Jersey.

"We'll need seven remote trucks," Scott read from his notes. "We'll have to lay out a floor plan for our building to include studio, VTR (Video Tape Replay) room, a couple of control rooms, and edit bays . . ."

Again I interrupted, "The people worry me. Let's try to figure out how many we'll need and start to put together an estimate of how much all this will cost."

Scott rode quietly making notes while I rambled on about trucks, people, equipment, the NCAA, etc. Then he came up with his estimate, "We'll need at least 80 people, a pretty good-sized building, and I don't know how much money. I do know we'll need a lot more money than Ed is working on right now."

"O.K., let's start thinking about how we'll present this to a bank or other investor. One thing we need is a positive national tie. I think we should pursue the NCAA as that hook. I'll call John Toner tomorrow, try the idea on him, and ask for his advice. He knows Walter Byers (Executive Director of the NCAA), and we can get to meet him, I'm sure."

I continued, "The next thing we need is a national name or two -- you know, Keith Jackson, Pat Summerall, Jim Simpson—someone of that stature."

"We ought to classify our needs," Scott suggested.

"Superstar, solid pro and journeyman. Dollars and cents I would estimate at about $200,000 for the big names, $75,000 to $90,000 for the solid pros and $25,000 to $40,000 for all the others."

"Got any ideas on how much a remote truck will cost us?" I asked.

"I dunno, maybe $600,000 to $700,000."

More excited than ever, I suggested, "Let's get to the format. I think we can do four or five half-hour sports roundups a day, and maybe 10 or 15 mini updates in and around events. One thing that always bugged me at WWLP-TV was that the sports segment never got more than 3 or 4 minutes on the air—nowhere near enough time to cover sports right. We won't let that happen."

"Seems to me the format's pretty basic," Scott said. "The games will be two or three hours long, and we'll put sports updates and sports roundups in between."

"Yeah, and we can show lots of sports that get little, if any, exposure on ABC's Wide World of Sports. Can you imagine college hockey on national TV, or volleyball, or swimming? I think there are sports enthusiasts by the millions that never get to watch their favorite sport on TV, and we're going to change all that."

Back in Connecticut at midnight, Scott and I were still making notes and asking questions. "Let's see what kind of a building we'll need," I suggested.

With that, we sat down at the kitchen table and began to lay out our thoughts for a building. Now, we're not architects, but that didn't stop us. For two hours, we played with a ruler and pencil and produced different floor plans before settling on one that very closely approximated what our architect later presented.

Scott remembers, "My father was hung up on how to squeeze all the room into the space he had drawn. Using a ruler, he laid out an 8″ by 12″ rectangle on a legal pad because everything could be scaled to one-eighths. Finally, I suggested that the building didn't have to be 64 feet by 96 feet. As a matter of fact, I pointed out that we didn't know where we would build it or if we could get approval for an uplink anywhere around central Connecticut, so finally we gave up and went to bed."

The idea was born, but what a rocky first few months of childhood lay ahead.

By 2 p.m. the next day, we had explained everything to Ed and he had quickly called the Bristol Redevelopment Authority to talk about the possible purchase of a piece of land in that tiny, quiet town. Ed called Bristol because our landlord, Jim Dovey, told us earlier in the day that he was putting his receive-only earth station in Bristol and thought they still had plenty of land left for sale.

I called John Toner early. "John, we've got an idea, and I'd like your advice. Can I see you today or tomorrow?"

"How about 9 tomorrow, Bill?" he asked.

"See you then!"

Friday, August 18
Storrs, Connecticut

"Good morning, John."

"Sorry I'm late. How are we doing?" Toner asked. He was referring to our progress on the UConn package and assumed my idea had something to do with that.

"Not all that well, but I think we have an idea that will help not only UConn, but the NCAA as well."

John's interest was evident, "Go on."

"Our idea is to make an arrangement with the NCAA similar to yours here at UConn and show events from schools all over the country all day long—not just prime time."

"Sounds interesting, but I don't know if it will work," he said.

"We want to try, and I need your advice on the way to approach the NCAA. Can you introduce us to Walter Byers?"

"Sure, but that's not where to start. First, I suggest you write all of this down, then get in touch with Tom Hansen, Walter's assistant. Tom will tell you how to proceed. The NCAA is very strict about television. The decisions are made by our Television Committee. Bo Coppedge, the Athletic Director at Navy, is the chairman. Let me know how you make out with Tom Hansen, and, if it makes sense, I'll arrange for you to meet Bo. Navy plays here on the 16th."

Encouraged by John's comments, I returned to Plainville to begin guessing what we could do for the NCAA and started to lay out our proposal.

"We have to make a first-class presentation," I told Ed and Scott. "Our first impression may be the only chance we'll have. I'll work with Guy (Guy Wilson, our printer friend at Lithographics, Inc.), and we'll come up with something. Ed, how are we doing with Bristol Redevelopment?"

"Bob Woods, their attorney that was here yesterday, needs some information from us, but he'll get us on the September meeting agenda. In the meantime, Sam (Sam Kasparian, Director of the Redevelopment Authority) told me he'll call if anyone else shows any interest in the lot we're after," Ed answered.

Our finances were in a woefully weak state by now. Our $25,000 loan request had been turned down by a local bank, and we needed cash.

"How about my relatives in Illinois?" I asked. "We'll have to give them some sort of an opportunity to buy stock if they lend us money, but that can't be all bad. I don't know if they can come up with anything, but you don't have any immediate prospects, do you, Ed?"

"No."

"Any other ideas on where we can find some financing?"

I asked.

No response from either Ed or Scott.

"I'll call my father." I did, and after a brief explanation, he said, "Why don't you come out the week after Labor Day and we'll talk about it."

Sounded good to us, so Scott and I made plans to fly to Chicago.

Friday, September 1
Plainville, Connecticut

Back in Connecticut, a phone message from Al Parinello was waiting. I called him immediately.

"Things are heating up," he said. "You'd better get that letter in the mail today (the letter confirming our transponder order). Send it Registered, Return Receipt Requested. There will be a real scramble after Labor Day, and I don't want you guys to lose your slot."

"Thanks, Al. The letter will go out today."

It's a good thing it did. As Parinello predicted, "things were heating up." An article in the *Wall Street Journal* shortly after Labor Day forecast an impending boom in the cable television business because of the advances made in satellite communications technology.

Wow! Al wasn't kidding! Suddenly requests for transponders were flooding RCA Americom's offices. Time, Inc. (owners of Home Box Office), Walt Disney Productions, Warner Communications and 20th Century Fox all applied. If the path to gold in the communications future was a transponder on RCA's "bird," the big boys wanted to stake a claim.

Fortunately for us, RCA considered requests for service on a chronological basis—first in, first on! When they announced the final Satcom I lineup at 2 p.m. on September 27, 1978, all of the companies listed were household names—except one: the E.S.P. Network of Plainville, Connecticut.

Hang on, I'm getting ahead of the story. On the financial side, we were really struggling! In desperation one night, I called Tom Cushman, a partner in K.S. Sweet Associates in King of Prussia, Pennsylvania. One of his responsibilities is the real estate management of the Farmington Woods Condominium Project where Scott and I lived.

Monday, September 11, 10:45 p.m. Avon, Connecticut

"Tom, this is Bill Rasmussen. I don't know if you can help me, but I know you move a lot of money into various investments. Maybe you could give me some advice and point me in the right direction. We've come up with an idea for an all-sports cable TV network distributed nationally via satellite, and we have to find a major investor."

After only a couple of minutes of explanation from me, Tom asked, "Can you call my office at 10 in the morning? There's someone I want to hear what you've just told me."

"Of course I'll call. Talk to you then. Thanks, Tom."

After a sleepless night, I was on the phone at 10 a.m. sharp.

"Tom, you asked me to call at 10 to tell my story to someone else. Is he there?"

"Bill, just a sec, I'll put you on the Speaker Phone. O.K., say hello to J.B. Doherty."

"Good morning, JB."

"Hi, Bill."

"Tell JB what you told me on the phone last night!"

So I did! I talked for 10 minutes without any comment whatsoever from the Speaker Phone in King of Prussia.

Finally, having gone through the entire plan, I was asked by JB, "Can you come down here tomorrow?"

"Sure, do you want me to bring Scott along?"

"Yes."

JB told us how to find his office and hung up.

Wednesday, September 13
King of Prussia, Pennsylvania

Scott and I quickly changed our Chicago plans to Thursday so that we could meet the mysterious JB Doherty on Wednesday as agreed.

The silver-haired, affable Tom Cushman greeted us and introduced JB. A pipe-smoking, intense ex-Marine captain, JB was all business. He immediately began taking notes as Scott and I explained our plans. As we completed our story, JB and Tom asked for a few days to digest what we had said and tentatively set another meeting for Wednesday, September 20th. Scott and I left for Chicago with very little more ammunition than we had before the King of Prussia meeting, but we were at least encouraged by the fact that our idea had not been rejected out of hand by the K.S. Sweet people.

Thursday, September 14
Chicago, Illinois

Meeting at my parents' home in suburban Chicago, Scott and I explained our project to my father and sister. He had always dreamed our family members would some day be in a business together. He definitely had no idea that that dream would involve cable TV and domestic communications satellites.

Sitting around the dining room table he asked, "If this is such a great idea, why isn't anyone else financing it?"

I answered, "We are going to talk to several people, including some major companies, but we need some interim cash, and I thought this might be the chance for the whole family to be involved in something that can be very successful."

Throughout the afternoon we discussed the E.S.P. Network. My sister joined us for part of the discussion and basically committed to help financially if my father did. I called my brother, Don, in Peoria, Illinois, that afternoon and gave him a brief explanation of what we were up to. He invited Scott and me to Peoria to discuss his possible participation. He, too, committed some dollars and expressed interest in playing an active role as an employee once the network was up and running. (Don ultimately did join the staff in July 1979.)

We left Illinois with enough borrowed cash to pay a few bills and hopefully stay afloat until October 1. We really needed to get a significant investor soon.

Saturday, September 16
East Hartford, Connecticut,
Ramada Inn

True to his word, John Toner told Bo Coppedge that I wanted to see him on Saturday before the UConn-Navy game.

"Just call Bo at the Ramada Inn in East Hartford Saturday morning. He's expecting your call."

Needless to say, I was at the Ramada Inn early Saturday and called Captain Coppedge's room.

"Bo Coppedge," he answered immediately.

"Captain, this is Bill Rasmussen. John Toner asked me to call you about our cable TV idea."

"Yes, yes he did. I'm a little busy now, but if you can wait, I'll meet you in the lobby in about 30 minutes."

"Fine!"

I sat in the lobby watching Navy's football players relaxing before the game, and suddenly the elevator door opened and Bo Coppedge was heading my way. Even though we had never met, it was easy for us to identify each other— we were the only civilians in the immediate area.

"Captain Coppedge?"

"Yes, Bill, pleased to meet you," he said in his friendly, Southern-gentleman style. "I understand you've got some ideas for us about cable TV."

"Yes, here's a summary." I gave him our *very* general outline—it was all we had.

"Bill, I'm going to study this, but I suggest you contact Tom Hansen at the NCAA and set up a meeting with him. Depending on when it is, I'll try and be there. Now you'll have to excuse me—my mind's on football. You call Tom and set something up, and we'll get this ball rolling."

End of meeting! I spent all of two minutes with the chairman of the NCAA Television Committee and wasn't sure that he had even heard me. Yet I had a good feeling about the Captain. Later I found that he not only heard me that Saturday morning, but proved to be a strong ally and gracious host whenever we appeared before the NCAA Television Committee.

Wednesday, September 20
King of Prussia, Pennsylvania

Allegheny Airlines had four very curious and interested passengers on their Hartford-to-Philadelphia flight at 7 a.m. Attorney Bob Hempstead joined Ed, Scott and me, and since we introduced him to the idea just before Labor Day, he had become an avid believer.

Arriving at K.S. Sweet's office, we were greeted by Tom and JB, and, following introductions for Eagan and Hempstead, immediately settled down in the conference room for a day-long discussion. The only interruptions of the day were for coffee and Tom's favorite "sticky buns" in mid-morning and some sandwiches brought in for lunch. We never left the room.

JB started the ball rolling, "Tell me the whole story again."

This time I had reinforcements, and I used them. Ed, Scott and Bob all joined in my explanation of what we had, what we needed and where we were going.

"Tom, where is all this leading us?" I asked. "Can we put something together?"

"We can't finance a project of this size, but perhaps we can provide some interim funding and help you write a business plan and look for major investors," he answered.

"I believe we can help in several ways," added JB. Before the day was over, we were all aware of JB's terse, concise, conservative and economical use of words. Throughout our association in the months ahead, he never changed.

Before the day was out, we had a letter of agreement with K.S. Sweet that:

1.   provided those much-needed interim funds, and

2.   provided help to write and present a business plan to potential investors.

As we were leaving, we found out why Tom and JB were able to make such a rapid decision. The afternoon that I had called Tom, he had been in the office of Andy Inglis, president of RCA Americom, finalizing a business arrangement. Talk about coincidence! Just hours before my call, Tom had heard from **RCA** Americom's top man many of the same facts, dreams, hopes and capabilities laying just ahead in the satellite communications business and the anticipated impact on the cable television industry.

The four of us headed back to Hartford to gather more information for our return to Pennsylvania the following week. We were under terrific pressure to provide **RCA** with some financial information and a detailed business plan by September 27—one week away.

Scott had already parried one call from the **RCA** comptroller's office asking some pertinent financial questions with, "Do we owe you any money? Have you sent us a bill that we haven't paid? Are you questioning our integrity?" Whoever called was so flustered we didn't get another call until after our agreement with K.S. Sweet was final. By then, we could talk business with some confidence.

Throughout the next week we were on the phone constantly with JB, supplying answers to his questions so he could prepare a business plan and represent to **RCA** that the E.S.P. Network was for real. During that week, Tom Cushman and/or JB made contact with **RCA** Americom Vice President for Finance, Dennis Elliot, and received assurances that we were, in fact, going to be announced on the 27th as one of the transponder lessees. Elliot also rescheduled our business plan presentation meeting from the 27th to

October 3rd in Washington to discuss our situation in greater detail. More on that later.

Frantic would be an accurate description of our actions for the next week.

The calendar moved toward the 27th, and, even though we had been tentatively reassured by JB's conversation with RCA, we were extremely nervous and anxious the morning of the announcement. We need not have worried. In late morning Ed Eagan took a phone call from Harold Rice, RCA Americom Vice President for Marketing.

"Congratulations, Ed, you've got your transponder. You'll be receiving a confirming Mailgram. Good luck!"

Ed hung up the phone and came straight out of his chair with a wild "We've got it!"

Scott and I jumped up, and, as Ed tried to relate the phone call, all three of us laughed, yelled, danced and jumped around like kids at a party. I can't describe our feelings of relief and elation.

That wasn't our final phone call of the day, however. In mid-afternoon, I answered the phone and an unfamiliar voice said, "I understand you have been awarded a transponder on the RCA satellite."

"Yes, we have," I answered cautiously.

"Well, I represent a New York firm that would like to make an offer for your company."

"Who do you represent?" I stalled.

"The name doesn't matter. We can make you a most attractive offer for your company right now."

Still basking in the euphoria of the earlier RCA call and positive that the caller knew something we didn't, I said, "Our company is not for sale. We're just getting started. Thank you for calling, though."

"Thank you," he said, and hung up.

Another round of jumping and dancing around our little office followed that call just as it had RCA's earlier call.

If somebody reacted that way that quickly after the announcement, we were now certain we could find some financing out there somewhere.

Inexorably, without a lot of help from us necessarily, but certainly with a lot of luck, the pieces were falling into place. The concept was struggling, but gaining strength. We had interim financing and our transponder, and we were scheduled to meet the NCAA in Kansas City in two weeks.

Chapter 5

The NCAA Cornerstone

Monday, October 2, 1978
King of Prussia, Pennsylvania

Flushed with transponder euphoria, we quickened the pace of our information gathering for JB Doherty. Our plan was to present appropriate assurances to RCA Americom's Vice President/Finance, Dennis Elliot, in Washington D.C., at our meeting Tuesday, October 3rd. Working through the weekend, we planned, analyzed, budgeted and guessed our way through a maze of information and questions to give JB and his partners some level of comfort about our idea. Monday I flew to Philadelphia to meet with the K.S. Sweet people to put the finishing touches on our material for the Elliot meeting.

Tuesday, October 3
Washington, D.C.

The Metroliner to Washington served as our meeting place as JB and I reviewed what had been accomplished in the two short weeks since our first phone conversation and how we would present it in D.C. We had explained our concept, acquired a transponder, were scheduled to meet with the NCAA, and decided we needed $10 million to launch our service. All of this was in a reasonably organized, typed form for presentation to Mr. Elliot. Not much substance, but pregnant with potential. We were so confident we even had a letter with us requesting a second transponder.

Noon, RCA Globecom

Dennis Elliot explained as he greeted us, "I'm in Washington for some FCC business with our international satellite division (Globecom), but am anxious to hear about the E.S.P. Network. You've certainly aroused our curiosity. I made reservations for lunch just around the corner."

Strolling leisurely to the restaurant on a gorgeous autumn day in the Capitol, I couldn't help but wonder if Dennis was going to tell us gently over lunch that RCA had reconsidered, and we didn't have a transponder after all. (Unknown to me, back in Plainville, Ed Eagan was about to receive the following mailgram dated October 3, 1978 from Al Parinello.)

```
MAILGRAM SERVICE CENTER
MIDDLETOWN, VA. 22645
```

```
1-006150C276 10/03/78 TLX RCAAMVASCO NYK NVNA
2 NEW YORK

MR. ED EAGAN
E.S.P. NETWORK INC.
319 COOKE STREET
PLAINVILLE, CONNECTICUT  06062


DEAR ED,          OCTOBER 3, 1978

WE ARE PLEASED TO CONFIRM YOUR ORDER OF SEPTEMBER 1, 1978 FOR
FULL-TERM PREEMPTIBLE SERVICE UNDER OUR TARIFF FCC NO. 1
FOR A 5 YEAR TERM STARTING JKNUARY 1, 1979 X  YOUR ASSIGNED
TRANSPONDER WILL BE NO. 7 ON F-1 X

WE WISH YOU THE VERY BEST OF LUCK AND LOOK FORWARD TO WORKING WITH
YOU X

IF YOU HAVE ANY QUESTIONS, PLEASE CALL ME X

VERY TRULY YOURS,

AL PARINELLO
RCA AMERICAN COMMUNICATIONS, INC.
60 BROAD STREET
NEW YORK, NEW YORK  10004

09:06 EST

MGMCOMP MGM
```

As we ordered, Dennis asked, "What is it you have in mind for programming your transponder?"

Alert to his use of the words "your transponder," I breathed a silent sigh of relief. At least until we proved otherwise, it seemed as if RCA considered us a customer.

JB and I had discussed our need to keep the NCAA portion of our plans very confidential so I answered, "We plan to do a variety of things all tied in with sports. We have some ideas about providing different kinds of coverage than are now found on the conventional networks."

"What about your financing? Is that all set?" he asked.

JB jumped in, "No, not really. We, that is, K.S. Sweet, have agreed to provide interim financing and to write a private placement memorandum seeking $10 million."

"Sounds fascinating," Elliot commented. "You should know that we're really interested in your success and want to help."

Hallelujah!! He wasn't asking for his transponder back at all—he wants us to succeed.

Dennis continued, "We believe that small, creative companies such as yours, should be given an opportunity to utilize this new technology. What kind of timetables have you established?"

JB was ready for that one, "We propose to complete the business plan with appropriate due diligence by the end of the month and begin making presentations November 1. While we don't anticipate an unqualified commitment by December 31, we do believe we will have a strong indication of interest from a major investor. Depending on how quickly that investor can move, we can conceivably have a tentative commitment by the end of the year. The key is to have the transponder in place.

"I plan to supply you with periodic progress reports and obviously with a copy of the business plan as soon as it's ready. We understand that if we are not making satisfactory progress, you can and will withdraw our rights to a transponder."

"Sounds ambitious, but I think we can live with that. You will have to keep me up to date, though. Even frequent phone calls will help."

We promised what he asked and enjoyed the fine lunch he had arranged. Walking back to Globecom, we all speculated a bit on the future of satellite/cable communications, but had no further conversation about E.S.P. Network other than a final, "Look forward to hearing of your progress," from Dennis.

As we left Globecom, JB and I had only a moment to congratulate each other on the successful meeting. He then headed for the Metroliner for Philadelphia, and I grabbed a cab to Washington's National Airport for the flight back to Bradley Field in Hartford.

Next up was our meeting with the NCAA in Shawnee Mission, Kansas. Since meeting Bo Coppedge in mid-September, Scott, Ed and I had been experimenting with different ways to utilize the tremendous programming potential offered by the NCAA, and how best to approach the Association with our plan. Both John Toner and Coppedge had spoken to Tom Hansen in Shawnee Mission when I called to set up the appointment.

All we had left to do in a week was to decide what to do for the NCAA and how to tell them we were going to do it.

I had scribbled a batch of ideas on a legal pad, and we called our friendly printer, Guy Wilson, for some creative presentation thought. With his usual aplomb, Guy ordered, "Leave it to me. I'll figure some *#&%$!! thing out and call you."

Next day he called, and I drove the ten miles to his plant in Canton, Connecticut, to review his suggestions.

Since he's the creative printer, I agreed quickly, especially when he said he planned to do it on very heavy, classy paper stock with a blue designed cover. The work accomplished in the next few days so impressed us that until well into 1980, when other people and other factors were involved, we never used any printer other than Guy. He selected the type for both the E.S.P. Network and later ESPN logos. He suggested layouts and colors and actually helped launch our massive mailing campaign that later paid off in universal cable industry acceptance.

Hold it! I'm doing it again—getting ahead of myself. Back to the NCAA presentation. The presentation was so well done and captured what we planned for the NCAA so vividly that it actually became the blueprint for the contract ultimately consummated between ESPN and the NCAA. Yet, it was simplicity personified!

After a frustrating wait for the few pages to dry sufficiently to be collated, Guy and I decided to personally prepare six copies for my trip to the NCAA. We carefully collated, checked and double-checked the copies, and he turned on a gadget that would punch the left edge for a comb binding.

"I'll get these punched, and then we'll put the comb* in, and you're all set," he said.

As I watched and we talked, he proceeded to punch **THE WRONG SIDE!!** So much for our six absolutely perfect sets. We collated six more sets without nearly the concern exhibited for the original sacred six copies, and he punched the right side this time. Then he dropped his next idea on me.

"I'm going to shrink-wrap** all six sets."

"Why?"

"Then when you hand them out, nobody can start reading until you're ready to talk to them. They'll all be trying to figure out how to open 'em!"

How could I argue that logic? I couldn't—he shrink-wrapped all six—even mine.

October 11, NCAA Headquarters Shawnee Mission, Kansas

"Yes, sir, may I help you?" asked the pleasant, cheerful lady behind the reception desk on the

---

* Plastic binding.
** Completely sealed in cellophane type wrapper.

top floor of the new, modern NCAA headquarters building.

"Yes, ma'am, Bill Rasmussen to see Tom Hansen."

"Oh, yes, he's expecting you. Come right this way."

Four steps around the corner, and I was seated in the conference room. "Thank you!"

"Hi, Bill, I'm Tom Hansen, and this is Dennis Cryder. Dennis is in charge of NCAA productions. I wanted him to sit in on this meeting. Bo Coppedge can't make it. We might as well hear what you have."

H'mmm!! The TV Committee Chairman didn't show up, and Walter Byers, NCAA Executive Director since 1951, wasn't even mentioned. Looks like my excitement on the phone when I arranged the meeting hadn't come through.

I gave Tom and Dennis copies of the presentation, and we briefly reviewed the contents.

"Bill, this really looks interesting, but as you know, we must work through our TV Committee with all proposals for any television coverage."

"Does that apply to cable?" I asked.

"Yes, it does. We really haven't done anything on the national level with cable, but if we do, it will have to be through the committee."

"How does the process work? Should I explain this concept to Mr. Byers?"

"No, we'll chat with him about it and show him your presentation," said Tom. "I suggest you write a letter to each member of the TV Committee. Send them a copy of this presentation. We'll schedule you for an appearance at our December 12 meeting. Then you can tell the committee members what you have in mind and what progress you have made."

Two months before I get to talk to anyone officially! "Tom, that's a long way off," I said. "Is there any way to speed up the process?" I was thinking of our commitments to RCA and K.S. Sweet. Frankly, I didn't know if they would still be with us if I couldn't come up with some NCAA announcement well before December.

"No, I'm afraid not," he answered. "We follow strict procedures. This is really a bad time of the year for us. We have the National Convention coming up in January in San Francisco, and we have an awful lot of work to do to prepare for that . . ."

I interrupted, "Assuming something can be done with you folks, how long do you think it will take to get an answer on the agreement?"

"About a year, and we'll have to have it approved by the membership. That would probably be at the 1980 convention if we go forward."

My heart dropped. There was no need to proceed if we couldn't even get approval for 15 months.

"Any way of speeding up the process?" I asked again.

"As I said a moment ago, not really, but getting started in December is a good idea. I recommend you come out and talk to the committee."

With sagging spirits, I answered Dennis's production-oriented questions as best I could, and before many minutes passed, was on my way back to the Kansas City airport for the flight to Hartford. The flight was a long one, or so it seemed. Buoyed with enthusiasm on the way to Kansas City the day before, I hadn't even considered anything less than a positive response. Heading home, deflated by the rather blasé reception and the long lead time factor, I began to contemplate possible moves to create enough excitement among the TV Committee members to shorten the anticipated long lead time.

By touchdown at Bradley Field, I had a battle plan:

1. Report the results to John Toner and enlist his aid. He knew the E.S.P. Network and its concept almost as well as we did.

2. Call Bo Coppedge and fill him in on the just-completed meeting and suggest he call Tom and Dennis.

3. Draft a letter to all TV Committee members as Tom had suggested and mail with presentation immediately.

4. Four days after mailing, call each committee member person-to-person and

volunteer to meet him anywhere to discuss our idea.

Back in Plainville, I met with Scott and Ed. We didn't produce any better ideas, so we plunged in, called Toner for an appointment and began gathering the proper mailing addresses for all the TV Committee members.

Monday, October 16
Storrs, Connecticut

John Toner was in particularly good humor as he greeted me, "Good morning, William, how goes the battle?"

"Good question, John! I was a bit surprised at the low key reception at the NCAA headquarters, but I'm doing the things Tom suggested."

"Good! I've talked to Tom, and they like your idea. Walter (Byers) is interested, but has his doubts about your ability to pull it off."

"I'll fly back to Kansas City and meet with him to answer any questions," I offered.

"No. Follow through on the mailings to the committee members . . ."

"They're already in the mail," I interjected.

" . . . and plan to go to that meeting in December."

Maybe I was a little hard on myself after the NCAA meeting with Tom and Dennis. John's comments renewed my resolve. However, he had touched on one very real NCAA concern: did we have the ability, both financial and creative, to "pull it off?"

John launched into another area. "Where do we (UConn) stand if all the NCAA programming becomes available?"

"That's an easy one," I answered. "Your entire contract will be incorporated as part of whatever package we put together." All of this was referring to our proposed agreement to carry a significant number of UConn athletic events for a period of three years with approximately 20-25 events in '78-'79, 30-35 in '79-'80, 40-45 in '80-'81. By now, we had abandoned the $18.00 season ticket plan and had, in fact, been counting on UConn as a key school in our first full year of NCAA programming.

We turned to an immediate problem. E.S.P. Network needed some cable credibility in a hurry. We had to come up with some "demo events" (i.e. demonstration shows to deliver to selected cable systems to illustrate our production capabilities). We needed those events soon. Still operating on a very restricted budget despite K.S. Sweet's commitment to advance funds, we were hoping to economize and do two events "back-to-back" and thus reduce crew and remote van costs.

"Will you allow us to originate a couple of events before the end of the year?" I asked.

"Basketball might be tough, but maybe we can work something out. What did you have in mind?" John asked.

"We'd like to combine a basketball game with one other event, either on the same day or on consecutive days."

"Would you consider soccer?" John was justifiably proud of his UConn soccer team. His coach, Joe Marrone, had built a national power that was on the threshold of challenging for a national championship, and a little TV exposure wouldn't hurt.

"Certainly," I answered, "but the season is almost over."

"You're right, but we will be host to an ECAC playoff game on Saturday morning, November 18, and we do have a basketball game the night before. We're playing an exhibition game with Athletes in Action."

Now we're cooking. "Sounds perfect," I said, "can we count on doing those two games? There's a lot of preparation with people, a truck and transponder time to order."

John warmed to the idea even more. "Yes, I think you can. I'll let you know tomorrow, but I don't anticipate any problems. We'll have to work very closely, though. Who will do the announcing?"

For years, radio station WTIC had covered UConn basketball, and two of the most popular announcers in southern New England had handled the broadcasts, Lou Palmer and Arnold Dean. They were good, and they were among John's personal favorites.

"How about Lou and Arnold?" I suggested.

"They'll be fine, but can you use them? They work for WTIC," John cautioned.

I wasn't certain, but I had known them both for a number of years and had also dealt with WTIC management while with the Whalers. I had a feeling we could make the necessary arrangements.

"All they can do is say no," I answered.

"Then let's try it," he said.

Back to Plainville. Ed and Scott both liked the idea. We still had time to contact several cable companies here and across the country to ask them to look at our efforts. We went to work to find a remote truck and called RCA to lease some transponder time because we would not have access to our transponder 7 until January 1, 1979.

In an interesting twist of fate, the transponder RCA assigned to us for November 17 and 18 was Madison Square Garden's transponder 9. It's ironic that the E.S.P. Network "demo weekend" events were transmitted on MSG's transponder 9 since today ESPN and MSG (they changed their name in 1980 to USA Network) are cable's biggest sports rivals.

Another plus to moving forward with our "demo events" was our October public appear-

ance before the Bristol Redevelopment Authority with a progress report. Ed and Scott worked
in concert with the Authority members between
meetings to keep them informed. The public
announcement that we planned to do the basketball and soccer games and had met with an
unidentified major program supplier added a
touch of believability to a few of the skeptics on
the Authority. However, we still had to convince
them we meant business. It seems their concern
was the same one we heard from all quarters
these days and one we had ourselves—what
about finances?

JB Doherty had come to Plainville to meet
with us and work on our business plan for Dennis Elliot at RCA. He was pleased that we were
going to do the two UConn events, but not so
pleased when he learned the cost. We also discussed hiring the people we would need and
decided that we were at the point of adding more
full-time people, not just part-timers. Past
associations had already identified three candi-
dates: Lou Palmer, Peter Fox and Bob
Ronstrom.

With the "demo events" on the immediate
horizon, Palmer, who carried the title Director of
Programming, and Peter Fox, our first Executive
Producer, went on the payroll November 15th.
Lou was at the first press conference back in
July and had followed our progress while ful-
filling his WTIC duties. By now, he was excited

by our progress and disappointed with his position at WTIC. Peter Fox came from a background in the advertising agency business with
strong emphasis on television production. Scott
and I had worked with Bob during his employment as the Whalers Comptroller. Later, he
moved to the WHA League office in Hartford.
He was anxious to try a new venture. Bob came
to the E.S.P. Network December 1st. All three
men would see ESPN go on the air, but only
Palmer would survive the massive changes that
occurred in 1979 and 1980. More on that later.

Well, now we were growing—our staff had just
doubled—and just in time. Lou and Peter took
charge of production details for our "demo weekend;" Ed worked on keeping the Bristol
Redevelopment Authority informed and
recruited cable systems for the games; Scott and
Bob worked on budgets and projections and were
closely involved with JB, and I continued the
NCAA quest by calling the TV Committee members and working with John Toner.

Those calls to the TV Committee turned out to
be enlightening, to say the least. I doubt if
there's a more non-committal group of men in
America. Take my call to Darrell Royal,
legendary football coach at the University of
Texas:

"Hello!"

"This is Bill Rasmussen from E.S.P. Network, calling to see if our presentation for a cable television package for the NCAA has arrived?"

"Yep!" Royal answered.

"Do you have any questions—can I fill you in on anything?" I asked.

"Nope!" was the answer.

"I look forward to seeing you in Kansas City on the 12th and hope we can make some progress toward a contract," I offered.

"Fine! 'Bye!" he ended the conversation.

Wow! Talk about non-committal! Talk about brief conversations!

Next up, Eddie Crowder, Athletic Director at the Universty of Colorado, an outstanding athlete in his earlier days.

"Hello, Bill. I received your letter and presentation! Thanks, it will help when we meet."

"Any questions I can answer for you?"

"No, thank you. Look forward to seeing you on the 12th."

"See you then. 'Bye!"

And so it went! No exorbitant phone bills talking to these guys. Polite, brief and totally non-committal. I wondered what our first face-to-face meeting would be like.

Helpless to do much more with specific TV Committee members, I joined Ed, Scott, Lou and Peter in "demo weekend" preparations. JB asked more questions. We began to interview other prospective employees and we worked furiously to contact "the right people" at various cable MSOs to encourage them to watch our initial efforts.

In addition to putting things in order for our upcoming UConn events, we plunged into preparations for our NCAA Kansas City meeting scheduled for December 12th. We gathered statistics, laid out a distribution map and planned a brief trip to Denver, Colorado.

The Denver trip was key to our early plans for pricing our service to the cable industry. Jim Dovey, our landlord, had told us of Gene Schneider's (president and CEO of United Cable Television) interest in new services to the industry. Jim also called Gene and told him to expect a call from me to discuss our new network. Dovey had paved the way well, and, when I called, Schneider came on the line immediately. We set our meeting for Monday, December 4th. This face-to-face contact with a major cable leader would make our life with JB a little easier and also give us some more ammunition for that NCAA meeting December 12th.

JB was active during these days, probing various possible investors for any indications of interest. He actually spoke with seven potential investors during November and early December. Armed with a more fully developed business plan and a private placement memorandum, he held comprehensive meetings with some. JB and I jointly met with one private investor, but frankly, the E.S.P. Network was not exactly the hottest item on anyone's future investment list in late 1978. The K.S. Sweet partners still had tremendous enthusiasm for the project, however, and backed up that enthusiasm with an expanded dollar advance after their initial $75,000 commitment was exhausted.

November 17-18
Storrs, Connecticut

Along with all the financial talking and planning, we still had some television work to do. E.S.P. Network's first telecast (the one on MSG's transponder 9) was set for Friday evening, November 17. The Telfax crew from Philadelphia (the same folks who "loaned" us a truck during the summer to show to the cable operators at our first meeting) was hired to do the remote origination. Peter Fox produced and directed the pre-game piece. I raced to New York City to complete arrangements for some computer animation for our logo and bring it back for the first event. Lou Palmer prepared for his play-by-play debut on the E.S.P. Network, and Ed and Scott worked right up to the last minute lining up cable companies to "preview" our 24-hour sports network. To be perfectly frank, I have no idea how many systems or subscribers saw our debut. Some system managers watched it in their offices, but refused to put it on their systems. Enough managers believed in us, though, to produce a gratifying—although meager—viewer response.

At half-time, Arnold Dean interviewed both John Toner and me. Of course, we spoke glowingly of the spectacular future for the E.S.P. Network, UConn sports, college and professional sports in general, and the great sports fans of Connecticut and the entire nation. The game itself wasn't much—really just an exhibition. But it was our first effort, and it came off surprisingly well.

Saturday at 10 a.m., the remote truck had been moved from the field house to nearby Gardner Dow Field for the Eastern Collegiate Athletic Association (ECAC) soccer match between UConn and Rhode Island. This wasn't as easy or successful as the basketball game because the camera locations were poor, but we did it and roared straight ahead with plans to do 20 to 25 more demo events for UConn after the first of the year.

We attracted enough interest with our "demo events" at the local cable level to receive a few calls asking for more. The cable press also made fleeting (but, to us, extremely important) note of our debut.

Tuesday, November 28
Piscataway, New Jersey

RCA was also interested in what we were doing, so JB and I found ourselves driving to Piscataway, New Jersey, for another meeting with Dennis Elliot. Up to this point, we had not told anyone about our specific plans with the NCAA, or even of our presentation delivered in October. Frankly, we were afraid someone with more resources would steal our idea.

Dennis ushered us into a cramped office and pleasantly asked about our progress. JB related his several investor contacts to date and gave Dennis the latest update of our business plan and then, turning to me, said:

"Bill has the most interesting news of the day, Dennis. At last he's going to tell you what we will use that transponder for."

Dennis smiled, "I've been wondering when we'd find out what you're up to."

Now it was my turn. "We've been very skittish about telling anyone until we were pretty well along, but here it is. I know you'll keep our confidence. We're going to contract with the NCAA to do 400 to 500 sporting events annually with at least one every day of the year. For 24 hours of sports, we've worked out a plan to charge the cable operators just a penny a day."

"Now that's quite a project," Dennis observed. "What do the operators think of your plan?"

"We haven't told them any specifics yet, just broad concepts. I'm going to Denver next week to meet with United Cable and should have a better idea when I return."

"How about the NCAA?"

"I was in Kansas City in October, and both JB and I will appear before the full Television Committee on December 12."

"That's great! There's plenty of work to do yet, but it seems as if you're heading in the right direction. We're patient and we want to see you succeed. Keep us informed and let's plan to get together in early January."

That was it. After some small talk, we were on our way back to King of Prussia, glowing with renewed faith in our plan. Dennis had barely examined the papers JB had delivered. He was more interested in our proposed usage and program service, and we almost got the feeling he was really rooting for us to make it.

In Plainville, lots of "blue sky" discussions were held virtually every day. To prove our plans were expanding, Peter Fox one afternoon proposed that we think of a new name. He wanted to see the word "global" or "world" or "international" incorporated, but in the end, we were still the E.S.P. Network.

Monday, December 4
Denver, Colorado

Leaving on the early flight to Denver from Hartford and working with the two-hour time difference from Eastern to Mountain, I was able to arrive in time for a late lunch with the United Cable people.

President Gene Schneider, one of the industry's pioneers in the '50's, was a leader in the new technology as well. He studied new ideas and services, and was known to be the first to sign for, promote and sell the latest idea. (In fact, he would become ESPN's first customer in March 1979.) Gene invited his Eastern and Western area Vice Presidents, Bob Ball and Harvey Boyd, to sit in to hear what I had to say over lunch.

"We plan to deliver a 24-hour sports service to the cable industry for just a penny a day," I announced enthusiastically. Not an eye even flickered. Here I had just announced this spectacular idea, and no one else at the table was visibly excited.

"It'll never work at that price," Harvey responded.

"Have you considered a pay sports service?" Gene asked.

"Why don't you become the industry's first totally ad supported network?" Bob threw in.

"Where will you get all the games?" Harvey again.

Suitably bombarded, I began to answer.

"Well, we've talked about pay, but we think a basic service should be more to the liking of the operators. It's simple, and since we plan 24 hours of service, you can just assign a channel on your system and never have to worry about switching from one transponder to another."

"Yes, but a penny a day is just too expensive," Schneider commented. "Bill, we're paying 10 cents for Ted Turner's Superstation, and all the new services want a nickel or a dime. We won't pay them, and you're talking 30 cents a month. It just won't work on that basis."

Bob Ball jumped back in, "I wasn't kidding when I suggested an ad supported channel. It won't be easy, but somebody's going to do it— why not you?"

Our discussion continued for another hour or so. Then it was time for me to head back to Connecticut. With a promise to consider all of their suggestions and come back to Denver later in the month with some revised thinking, I thanked all three men and drove to Denver's Stapleton Airport.

The suggestion and comments of these respected cable people were passed on to Ed, Scott and JB. Throughout the week, we tried different ideas and formulas on each other. Obviously, our original idea would have to be altered. While the debate continued, however, I had to prepare for a trip to Annapolis, Maryland.

Friday, December 8
Annapolis, Maryland

Bo Coppedge had proposed a meeting at the United States Naval Academy before my appearance in Kansas City on December 12th. He was very helpful and suggested that I bring as many visual aids as possible along with more presentations.

"Bring along your financial helper too," he instructed. "You'll really like the boys on the committee, but they'll have lots of questions for you."

"That's fine by me," I answered. "How long will I have, and will any decisions be reached?"

"We'll make sure you have all the time you need, but we won't reach any decisions. Tom Hansen will summarize your proposal and circulate it to the Executive Council. There'll be some talk to key people at the national convention in San Francisco in January, and, if it looks promising, we'll probably invite you back to Kansas City for our February meeting. The January meeting will be held during the convention in San Francisco, but there are just too many things on the agenda to consider your proposal until February. Great idea you have, Bill, really great, and I'll make sure you get a good hearing before the committee."

I thanked him, left and headed for Baltimore's Friendship Airport. Along the way, I called JB's office only to discover he had gone to Princeton,

New Jersey, for the day on business, but he had left a phone number for me to call after 10 p.m.

When I called, JB politely inquired about my Navy visit. Knowing I was heading for Kansas City on Monday, he said, "How would you like to detour through Los Angeles on your way to Kansas City?" (Since my trip would start from Hartford, Connecticut, that was going to be quite a detour.)

"Sure! Why?"

"Got a pencil? Take this name and number down. Stuart W. Evey—that's E-v-e-y, Vice President, Getty Oil Company, 3810 Wilshire Boulevard."

"Getty Oil Company? What am I supposed to do? Will you be there?" I asked.

"No. Tom Cushman and Stu have had some Hawaii dealings in the past, and when Tom called, Stu said our cable idea was worth listening to. No commitments, of course, but Getty does have a variety of investments, and Stu's the man in charge of their non-oil investments."

"What shall I take?"

"Yourself, mostly! You can answer all of his questions a lot better than I can. You should leave one of our presentations with him, though."

"Sounds good, but you don't sound very optimistic," I observed.

"You never know, but it's worth the time. If it's something that fits, they have the money. We'll see what happens. Good luck!"

"Thanks, JB. I'll call you from L.A. as soon as I leave the meeting."

Chapter 6

The Getty Connection

Monday, December 11, 1978
Los Angeles, California

As I paid the taxi driver, I had no idea of what to expect when I walked through the doors to the security checkpoint of the Getty Building. I was directed to the 18th floor, where Mr. Evey was expecting me. Stepping off the elevator, I found myself in the tightly secured reception area of the corporate headquarters of the giant oil company. The receptionist's phone call to the inner sanctum produced Mr. Evey's secretary who escorted me to his office.

A gracious, impeccably attired, tall, slender man, about my age, greeted me warmly. "Bill, Stu Evey! Glad you could make it. Say hello to Wendel Niles. Wendel is a producer here in Hollywood, and, since what you have is a little bit out of our area of expertise, I've asked him to join us to help me understand your project."

"Nice to meet you!"

"Would you like some coffee?" Stu asked. His secretary took orders for all three of us. "Tom (Cushman of K.S. Sweet) tells me you have an exciting project that Getty should explore."

"Well, I think it's very exciting. The opportunity exists to provide a service not available to cable operators today. If we move quickly, we'll preempt others who may be considering the same thing. Half a dozen people have already tried our idea, but their timing was wrong. What makes us different is our RCA transponder on Satcom I and a proposed arrangement with the NCAA."

"Let's hear some details," Stu prodded.

For the next 30 minutes, I recounted what had transpired from June to this meeting: the RCA transponder story, the UConn pay package idea, the interim arrangement with K.S. Sweet, and the NCAA contact. I finished with a brief summary of the financial information and require ments which were detailed in the material I was going to leave with them.

"E.S.P. is looking for $10 million—5 in equity and 5 in long-term debt. Our pressing need at the moment is at least to have an indication of interest by December 31. That's the next deadline we have to meet for RCA; besides, K.S. Sweet will have reached their limit as far as interim financing goes."

Evey listened closely and asked plenty of questions. "Well, I can't say anything until our financial people analyze your proposal. Even if we move forward, it will take longer than the deadline you're under. However, I am interested in learning more about the idea."

A major breakthrough! No previous potential investor had shown even this faint flicker of interest. Throughout the meeting, Mr. Niles contributed little because, as he admitted, he knew virtually nothing of cable TV. Silently, I hoped he wouldn't dampen Evey's interest with some blundering statement after I left. Luckily, he didn't.

Evey and I exchanged the usual good-byes and "We'll-be-in-touch" amenities; by 10 a.m., I was back on Wilshire Boulevard hailing a taxi to Los Angeles International Airport.

Unknown to me, almost before I reached the ground floor and walked off the elevator, Evey had started the wheels turning. He called his financial manager, George Conner, and . . . I'll let George tell you what happened:

"Rasmussen made a pitch to Stuart W. Evey, Vice President of Getty's Diversified Operations Division at 9 a.m. at the oil giant's Los Angeles Corporate Headquarters. My involvement began about one minute after Bill left Evey's office. Evey called and said he had an investment opportunity for me to look at. After I read through the proposal for nonstop sports on cable television, I told Evey that I thought the proposal looked interesting enough for us to proceed with further evaluation. He told me ESPN had to have an answer no later than December 31, or the company would probably go under. We knew it would take longer for us to evaluate a business opportunity in an area new to Getty. However, we might know we *didn't* want to invest by the deadline. Because of the rush, I delayed my Christmas vacation in Tulsa to begin learning about earth stations, preemptible and protected transponders, Nielson ratings, and the NCAA Television Committee."

Meanwhile, I was flying to Kansas City to meet JB. We were scheduled to make our first appearance before the NCAA Television Committee.

Tuesday, December 12
Kansas City, Missouri

Dennis Cryder, NCAA Director of Productions, greeted JB and me outside the TV Committee meeting room at the Kansas City Airport Marriott Hotel.

"Good morning, Bill. Welcome to Kansas City."

"Morning, Dennis. I'd like you to meet J.B. Doherty. JB is a partner in K.S. Sweet Associates, our investment banker."

"Nice to meet you, JB."

"What's our schedule?" I asked.

"The committee is taking care of some routine business and will take a coffee break about 8:45.

Bo will come out and invite you in during that break."

And that's exactly what happened. Bo Coppedge greeted us warmly, then informally introduced both JB and me to several members of the committee during the break. Tom Hansen came over to say hello; again, Walter Byers was nowhere in sight. I began to think I'd never meet him. Bo maneuvered us to the front of the room, and we cued our demonstration tape. (This was a specially produced, five-minute tape to explain visually some highlights of our proposal). We mounted a $3' \times 4'$ map of the United States showing current cable system locations, and Captain Coppedge called the meeting to order.

The conference room at the Airport Marriott was set up with tables in a rectangle. From our vantage point at the front of the room, Tom Hansen, Eddie Crowder, Bob Moorman and Cryder were seated on our right; Cecil Coleman, Bob Seiple, George McCarty and Carl Maddox on our left; and directly in front of us sat Darrell Royal with an empty chair on each side of him.

In his gracious manner, Bo introduced both JB and me to his committee members. To my surprise, I noticed Walter Byers had arrived and taken the empty chair to the left of Royal. Listening to Bo's introduction, I must admit that I was momentarily intimidated by the sight of these two powerful men facing me. Stern, sincere Royal, arms folded across his chest, studied us with a noncommittal look. Even more imposing, the fabled NCAA czar, Byers, with his shock of white hair and equally impassive expression, waited for my presentation. Bo concluded his brief summary and introduction of us with, "... and now I'm going to ask Bill to explain his idea."

"Thank you and good morning. I'm delighted to have the opportunity to discuss with you an exciting new idea that will give your member institutions greater TV exposure and also earn a few more dollars for them as well. We've been working with the idea every hour of every day, and I'm sure I'll miss some things, so please ask questions as we go along."

I told the same story I had related the day before to Stu Evey in Los Angeles. I must admit that I dropped in the fact that I had visited Getty Oil and anticipated no problem financing our project. JB answered the financial questions as they arose, and, generally, our presentation went well. Here we were, two rookies, JB and me, telling these NCAA heavyweights what a great thing we were planning to do for NCAA sports, and we didn't even hesitate.

The reception of our presentation by the committee was polite and courteous. They asked questions with Crowder and Coleman leading the way while Tom Hansen recorded the proceedings. Neither Byers nor Royal said a word, but the committee appeared more than a little interested. As Bo had told me in Annapolis, no decision was reached. We didn't even get invited to another meeting. As JB and I finished, Bo Coppedge asked, "Any more questions for these fellas? No? O.K! Well, Bill and JB, on behalf of the committee, I want to thank you for being with us today. You've got a great idea, and you did a great job of bringing us up to date. Tom will be in touch with you."

As JB and I headed for the airport, we debated our effectiveness before the committee and decided we had done all that could be done. Nothing had been left out, and the members certainly received plenty of food for thought. Next stop: Denver and five MSO meetings.

Wednesday, December 13
Denver, Colorado

Our plan in Denver was to talk to as many people at high levels as possible to evaluate their reactions so we could formulate a sensible plan for system participation. JB was only going to stay with me for one day; then, I was scheduled to go on to several other cities for similar meetings.

While I was in Denver, Ed Eagan was making a similar tour to about a dozen medium-sized MSOs and independents from Massachusetts to Texas.

Back in our makeshift office, Scott and Bob Ronstrom were totally occupied in our "crisis control center," the name they applied to their daily task of confronting the questions and problems posed by nervous employees and creditors. We were woefully thin on cash and managing "crisis control" was no mean task.

I soon discovered that when Getty investigates something, they really investigate! George Conner was already in tune with us. Well, maybe not quite in tune, but he at least caught up with us at a hotel via telephone to start asking serious questions. Every day for nearly three months, I spoke with George (although on December 13, we still hadn't met) from airports, car rental agencies, hotels, phone booths on street corners, etc. Unknown to me, every time I said I met with a cable MSO or RCA or the NCAA, Getty called the same people to determine what they thought of our idea. Getty was obviously serious!

First stop for JB and me in Denver—ATC— American Telecommunications—one of the largest MSOs in the country. Chip Morris and Greg Powers, two corporate programming executives, greeted us cautiously. "We understand you intend to do sports 24 hours a day. How much will it cost?"

"We think a penny a day per subscriber should be reasonable, but we'd like to hear your thoughts," I answered.

We discussed our idea for about 30 minutes; for some undefinable reason, both JB and I were down as we left the meeting. Something wasn't right, but we couldn't quite put our fingers on it. Oh, well, next stop, Daniels & Associates.

Tom Johnson and Jean O'Grady listened to our pitch with barely concealed humor.

"You'll never get a penny a day," Tom told us.

"Once you figure out what you're going to do, get back to us," Jean suggested. Years later, they both told me that after JB and I left, they enjoyed a good laugh, never expecting to see or hear from us again.

Back at the hotel, JB and I reviewed our day's meetings and decided we had to make a drastic change in our presentation. No one seemed the slightest bit interested in our "penny-a-day" theory. Before JB had to leave for the airport, we decided to try a new approach. We would become primarily advertiser supported with greatly reduced fees to the operator. My first stop the next day would find some gratification in our new plan—I was scheduled for a United Cable meeting at 9 a.m.

Thursday, December 14

At United Cable, Gene Schneider, Bob Ball and Harvey Boyd could hardly believe their ears. The ideas they proposed just ten days ago were now roughly the E.S.P. Network's new plan.

"I've also been to see Getty Oil and the NCAA, and we're really starting to cook," I added.

I handed them a single piece of paper outlining our proposed studio and remote facilities plus our plans for building a 108 person staff.

"If you pull this off, I want to be your first affiliate," Gene Schneider said.

"I'll hold you to that," I laughed.

"That's fine!" he answered. "We need more of these kinds of things."

On that encouraging note, I drove around the corner to TCI–Telecommunications, Inc.–headquarters in another part of the Denver Technological Center. Graham Moore, Vice President of Programming for this huge MSO, greeted me. "Coffee?" he asked. Graham was a broadcast veteran, and we had many things in common, right down to the way we parted our hair—with a face cloth.

Listening to my explanation of my MSO meetings, Getty and NCAA contacts, he said, "I like the concept very much. This is something TCI will be interested in, but frankly, I don't see how you can pull it off. No ad supported service exists, and you'll need a ton of money. Doing your own production is expensive too. I wish you well, but I don't think you can do it."

Talk about emotional highs and lows. Coming on the heels of my positive United Cable visit, Graham's comments confirmed his interest, but, at the same time, he flat-out said it'd never happen.

Wearily, I headed for the airport and my next stop, Austin, Texas.

Friday, December 15
Austin, Texas

Scheduled to meet Greg Liptak of CPI, Community Properties, Inc., I called our office in Connecticut to find that George Conner was looking for me. Renting a car, I drove to the nearest phone booth and once again answered the same old questions from George.

"What did the Denver MSOs think? Anybody sign any agreements? Tell me again about TV ratings! Any later news from the NCAA? I know I'm asking the same questions over and over. I simply have to learn a lot about your business in a short time because the deadline you've given us for a decision is so near."

On a hunch, I called CPI headquarters to confirm my meeting with Greg. His secretary apologized because Greg had been called out of town and wouldn't be back for the rest of the day. She hoped this wouldn't inconvenience me too much.

I guess it just depends on your interpretation of inconvenience. I had flown from Denver to Dallas to Austin and rented a car, which I now returned with just four miles used to the car rental agency, and flew back to Dallas. Obviously, the stop in Austin hadn't gone as well as Denver.

Monday, December 18
Dallas, Texas

Met with Jim Whitson, President of Sammons Communications, another major MSO.

"You've really got something here," Jim encouraged me as he heard my now-standard pitch. "We'll have to look at our channel capacity in each of our systems, but if you make it happen, you've got a customer."

Buoyed by this response, I quickly reported to George at Getty headquarters and left for Atlanta.

Tuesday, December 19
Atlanta, Georgia

One good and one bad meeting here. Ernie Olsen, Vice President at giant Cox Cable, was positive, enthusiastic and the first guy who really seemed to believe we had a shot at making the whole thing work.

John Janos at Rollins, an MSO more interested in electronic gadgetry than in new programming and marketing, was late for our meeting and gave no encouragement whatsoever. After waiting 30 minutes in his tiny office, I felt I received a standard "we're not interested in anything new" response and left. Being an optimist, I decided Ernie was 100% on target, and John wasn't smart enough to recognize a good thing when he saw it. I flew to Norfolk, Virginia, in a good mood.

Wednesday, December 20
Norfolk, Virginia

Great meeting with some fine gentlemen here. Dick Roberts, President of TeleCable, and Gordon (Red) Herring, Vice President, Operations, were gracious hosts with soft, unhurried Southern drawls, although Dick is a Massachusetts native. They received our plan well. They agreed to evaluate the project and determine where sports would fit into their 1979 plans as they added programming to their upgraded systems.

I placed the mandatory call to George Conner. Then I dialed JB since I hadn't talked with him for four days, and I assumed he would be a little nervous by now. Getty was moving forward with strategy committee meetings and computer analyses. By its corporate standards, it was moving quickly; from our point of view, Getty was ponderously slow. However, E.S.P. Network was spending money faster than JB liked. He, too, was engaged in daily communications with George, yet we still hadn't met him. JB and I had obviously talked about this "Getty man" and agreed he seemed very competent. We wondered if we'd get along in person as well as we did on the telephone. Little did I realize what close friends we'd become. Both mentally and physically weary after two weeks, I still had one more stop—New York City.

Friday, December 22
New York City

Two of the biggest MSOs—Teleprompter and Warner—are located here. As you might expect, it's pretty tough to sell anything to Manhattanites without facts. The meetings went well, but I received nowhere near the "quasi-commitments" I had from other systems in the past several days. Meeting at their midtown corporate headquarters, I answered question after question at both companies. In the end, neither one encouraged me as their Colorado compatriots had, but merely asked to be kept informed. Oh, well, can't win 'em all.

I called Tom Hansen at NCAA headquarters to tell him the results of my meetings: five quasi commitments; two "keep us informed;" one "get back to us;" one "no comment;" one did not keep appointment; one not interested. Tom was very pleased with the results and asked about the financing.

"Getty is working very closely with us," I truthfully responded. "One of their problems is the length of time it will take to get a commitment from the NCAA."

"I can understand that," he said. "I don't know if we can speed things up, but I'll tell Walter of your progress with the systems, and we'll talk about it in San Francisco. I'll be staying at the Fairmont; please keep me up to date with developments."

Time for my Conner call.

"George, the NCAA is very pleased with our MSO response. The MSOs I talked to yesterday and today are about the same as all the others—we've got customers if we ever get on the air."

"Great! Bill, what are you doing next Wednesday or Thursday? I'd like to meet you and JB in Chicago and have you talk to someone."

"Tell me when, and I'll be there," I quickly replied.

"Let's meet at the O'Hare Hilton. How's 10 a.m. next Thursday sound?"

"Fine, I'll tell JB, and unless you hear from me, we'll see you on the 28th."

Back to Connecticut for the Christmas holidays. Even though our December 31st deadline was closing in, I had the feeling something positive would happen to keep us alive. As I walked into the office, I chuckled. The Plainville troops had scrawled an impromptu "potential subscriber scoreboard" on a convenient window. It wouldn't pay the bills, but it made us all feel good.

Thursday, December 28, O'Hare Hilton
Chicago, Illinois

The "someone" George wanted us to meet was Dr. John Gartley of the Northwestern University School of Communications. John was very correct and proper in his questioning of JB and me, but frankly, since technology had been moving so rapidly and he was in an academic, rather than a business environment, his information was quite far out of date.

We later discovered the real reason for the meeting was not so much to gather information, but to let George meet us and do a first-hand, face-to-face evaluation of JB and me. Getty also was interested in Dr. Gartley's personal evaluations of us. For our part, we were pleased to finally meet the face that went with the phone voice we had gotten to know so well during the past three weeks. George's cherubic visage combined with his straightforward, no-nonsense approach to business left us in a quandary. On the one hand, he was friendly and enthusiastic, while on the other, he cautioned us not to expect too much from Getty too soon.

This meeting culminated a frantic month of activity for JB and me along with Scott, Ed and all the others operating out of Plainville. It also had been quite a month for George, as he explains:

"For three solid weeks I asked a lot of questions of a lot of people: producers, directors, sports commentators, advertising agency personnel, cable television system owners, and everyday people I came in contact with at airports, hotels, anywhere. What do you think about sports on television 24 hours a day? What sports do you enjoy? How often would you watch? At the same time, Evey was asking his own questions. Between us we wanted to know as much as we could about the potential of a cable television network.

"As expected, we were not ready to proceed on any basis by the December 31, 1978, deadline. We had learned enough to know the proposal deserved further business and financial evaluation. The project seemed to have significant potential; however, there were many unknowns. There were no Nielsen ratings for cable television. How many people would watch reruns of Saturday college football games on Sunday and Monday? ESPN was hoping to strike a deal with the NCAA Television Committee for rights to a wide variety of collegiate events. A big concern was the point at which sponsors would be willing to advertise on ESPN; that would be the main revenue source. And what if the satellite stopped working?

"ESPN was told that Getty was interested in a possible investment, but that another 30 to 45 days was needed for evaluation. ESPN would have ceased to exist during that time had it not been for a few people, including me, who believed it was one hell of an idea."

Those are George's comments in retrospect. On Friday, December 29, 1978, Evey's response to JB's inquiring phone call was, "If you have to have an answer today, it's 'No.' Can't K.S. Sweet fund this project a little longer? You know we're interested, but we're not ready for any positive decision yet."

So that's it. Our deadline arrived, and we had no financial commitment. 1978 ended on a down note. However, strategy for ultimate success evolved in December. We didn't recognize it at the time, but the strategy that emerged from that whirlwind time was really simple: tell the investor (Getty) of the NCAA and MSO enthusiasm; tell the NCAA of the investor (never mentioning Getty) and MSO enthusiasm; and tell the MSOs of the NCAA and (no name) investor enthusiasm. We continued to employ that strategy through January and February.

Tuesday, January 2, 1979
King of Prussia, Pennsylvania

December 31 had come and gone, and we were still alive. Meeting with Tom and JB at K.S. Sweet, I got assurances that we would survive at least a little while longer.

"Getty just may do this," Tom offered. "I don't think we should give up just yet. The NCAA news is encouraging, and the systems seem interested enough. What are you planning to do now?"

"I'm scheduled to fly to San Francisco tonight, then to San Diego, and I'll be back in New York City on Friday."

JB was getting ready to update RCA's Dennis Elliot; although we didn't have very much concrete evidence, at least we were now able to talk about individual people, systems, and Getty Oil. That's progress!

With assurances that K.S. Sweet would continue to fund, I was off to the West Coast. Ed Eagan continued his system operator missionary work with a visit to the Mid-Central Cable Show.

Our new Vice President of Marketing after 24 years as advertising manager for Connecticut General Life Insurance Co., Bob Chamberlain, and I planned to meet and interview Bob Jeremiah at the San Francisco Airport at 9 p.m. Pacific Time. We were looking for a consultant, and Chamberlain claimed Jeremiah was one of the advertising community's great "numbers geniuses." Since Getty was looking for some projections on advertising and audience penetration, we needed help. We completed our San Francisco meeting with Jeremiah, who agreed to work on a summary ratings model for us. Chamberlain and I continued on to San Diego.

Thursday, January 4
San Diego, California

Ektelon, manufacturers of raquetball equipment, was the reason for this trip. Chamberlain had discovered they were planning a nationwide promotion centered around a tournament. The company wanted us to buy its package for our all-sports network. This proved to be the first of thousands of calls and proposals for similar

ideas. After all, promoters reasoned, E.S.P.
Network needed lots of programming to fill 24
hours a day.

Bob stayed on the West Coast while I flew to
New York City for a scheduled meeting with
Major League Baseball to discuss possible
weekly cable coverage. That meeting never happened. However, I had a second round of discussions with Teleprompter and Warner. I
sandwiched in a public relations type phone call
to Dennis Elliot at RCA and called Plainville to
learn the latest from the "crisis control center."

Scott told me a couple of meetings had been
scheduled, including one with the North American Soccer League (NASL); we were getting
quite a bit of attention from the cable trade press
looking for interviews, and UConn's business
office wanted to talk about our contract. Bristol's Redevelopment Authority was also becoming suspicious since we hadn't arranged our
financing yet. Oh, yes, and we were out of
money. Time to call JB . . . again!

The next couple of weeks were loaded with
emergency phone calls, informational calls to and
from George Conner, and one very interesting
call from Tom Hansen asking me to come to
Kansas City for a special NCAA TV Committee
meeting on January 25.

Dennis Elliot at RCA was becoming a little
impatient, so JB and I scheduled a meeting on

January 24. We invited George to join us at that one.

On the production side of things, E.S.P. got to use its very own transponder for the first time on January 9th when we originated the UConn-Rutgers basketball game from Storrs. We even received assurances from several systems around the country that they would carry the telecast.

Things were indeed heating up. We still had only 10 employees, including 2 secretaries, but we were doing a live telecast, scheduled to meet both RCA and the NCAA on consecutive days, feeding Getty answers to all their questions, and now Bob Chamberlain added a new dimension. Without any studio, long term financing nor any commitment from the NCAA, Bob approached Anheuser-Busch, brewers of Budweiser, about becoming an E.S.P. charter advertiser.

"Gene Petrillo at D'Arcy, McManus wants to meet with us," he announced in mid-January. "Gene is the top agency man for Budweiser and wants to hear our story."

So, on the 15th we told our story again—this time to our very first advertising contact. The pieces were really falling into place, but no one was making any long-range commitments.

Gene asked, "Do you have any proposal for me?"

We didn't, but promised to get back to him shortly with something in writing. We delivered our proposal the next day.

"We propose to sell 1/8 sponsorships in our network for $2,760,000," Bob disclosed to Gene. "You'll have billboards and 30-second spots throughout the day."

"What about exclusivity?" Gene queried.

"We can consider that, depending upon your commitment," I answered.

We chatted for a few more minutes, and Gene promised to call us later in the week. Thursday he called and said he wanted to see us again on Monday.

Monday, January 22
New York City

"I've talked to my people at the brewery," he opened, "and we'd like to buy a franchise position for a half million dollars."

Bob and I looked at each other. We assumed Gene would come back with a counter offer, but not one-fifth of what we were asking.

Bob said, "We'll have to think about that one. Can we get back to you in a few days?"

"Sure!"

"I don't think we can give you all that time and certainly not exclusivity at that price level," I added.

"Well, let's talk when you're ready."

Bob and I left Gene's office; as we hit the street, we decided we would say no to the $500,000 counter proposal. How about that? Our company was almost broke, yet we're brash enough to say a half-million-dollar offer isn't good enough.

Scott had been in California for a week. When he called, we compared notes on the progress of events on both coasts.

"I've been talking to Bob Seidenglanz at Compact Video," he said. "These guys are all right. They'd like to build our remote fleet and do the design work for our studio facilities."

"That's fine, Scott, but if we don't get some money soon, it's all academic."

I told him about our Gene Petrillo/Budweiser meetings and those upcoming with Dennis Elliot and the NCAA. A "no" answer from any of the three would doom E.S.P. before it got off the ground. Yet, Scott wasn't the slightest bit discouraged.

"Can you come to L.A. after your Kansas City meeting with the NCAA?" he asked. And I thought I was an optimist!

"Sure, why?"

"I think you should meet the Compact Video people and talk about our proposed remote trucks."

"O.K., where are you staying? Book a room for Thursday night for me."

"Great, see you some time Thursday, Dad." Then he hung up.

Tuesday morning, January 23, I raced out to UConn to meet with John Toner before heading south for that Dennis Elliot meeting.

"William, the committee really likes your idea," he started. "As you know, I'm on the council, and Tom Hansen has sent me a summary of all the recent discussions. Your E.S.P. Network is very definitely in the running for a cable contract, and—and here's the good news for you—*the committee decided at the convention last week to move rapidly.* If a decision is needed, they will poll the member institutions and move this project along quickly."

I was stunned! Happily stunned, that is! What great news! Then I remembered something else John said about being one of two companies making our appearance before the committee on Thursday.

"Who else is bidding?" I asked.

"I can't tell you that, Bill, but rest assured, you're very much in the running."

I almost didn't need an airplane to fly to Philadelphia to meet JB and George. When I arrived, I couldn't tell them the good news fast enough.

Wednesday, January 24
Piscataway, New Jersey

Our meeting at RCA was a classic example of high-level corporate sparring. George Conner, representing Getty, was trying to find out just how far RCA would go with our transponder lease without a major financial commitment, while Dennis Elliot was poking around trying to discover just how real Getty's interest in us was. JB and I merely tried to keep the conversation alive with positive comments about our upcoming meetings with the NCAA and Budweiser, along with the continued positive MSO response.

George, JB and I left Dennis feeling that we still had some time, but that our days were definitely numbered. We needed a big-money partner—and soon. With this newly perceived pressure from RCA, we left for the Philadelphia airport and our flight to Kansas City.

Fog shrouded the airport, and there was some doubt about our ability to find an outbound flight to make that scheduled NCAA meeting. Wouldn't that be something? On the threshold of a decision and fogged in in Philadelphia, of all places.

To entertain ourselves, JB, George and I raced from airline to airline and changed connections a few times from TWA to United to Braniff and back to TWA. It didn't make any difference which airline—we just wanted to get under way. After four hours at the TWA gate, George was intimately familiar with all the internal airline phone numbers to check luggage, weather, reservations and who knows what else. At one point, he strolled to a vacant TWA counter to use the phone and, instantly, about eight other passengers formed a line in front of the counter to ask him questions. Undaunted, he fielded them all, as JB and I howled with laughter from

the other side of the gate area. We were a bit
punchy, and it didn't take much to amuse us, I
guess. It was quite a sight, though, to see the
serious, conservative, almost shy Mr. Conner
playing ticket agent. He never did tell us what
he said to all those people, but I know he was
awfully anxious to leave after his performance.
And leave we did, finally, about 9 p.m.

Thursday, January 25
Airport Marriott
Kansas City, Missouri

Upon our arrival at the NCAA TV Committee
meeting room, Dennis Cryder welcomed us as he
had in December. I introduced George,
"...*from Getty Oil* ." We also found out that
the other bidding company was ATC—the first
MSO JB and I had visited in Denver last month.
Now we knew why they had been so cautious in
their reception of us—they were competing for
the same contract! Just 30 feet away, inside the
meeting room, ATC was making its pitch.

I couldn't understand the NCAA's dilemma.

Since ATC was an MSO, obviously some other
MSOs would find it difficult to do business with
them should they be awarded an NCAA contract. We later discovered their proposal called
for 100 live nightly events during the school
year, which further confused the issue. In our
eyes, the TV Committee was comparing apples

and oranges—our full-time service with their part-time service.

Suddenly the committee room doors opened, and Bo Coppedge was again inviting us in for coffee. This time we felt more assured than that first time around, and we had an unknown secret weapon—George Conner! As JB and I shook hands with everyone, we introduced George by his exact title—the Financial Manager of Getty Oil's Real Estate and Forest Products Division—no more, no less! Amazingly, not one person asked a direct question about George's presence at the meeting, or even his association with E.S.P., and after a few minutes, Captain Coppedge called the meeting to order.

"Bill, you know everyone here, why don't you introduce your friends. We know JB, of course."

"Thanks, Bo. For those of you who haven't met him, this is George Conner, the Financial Manager of Getty's Non-Oil Division." That's all I said—no further explanation. First, there was nothing else to say; and second, even though we hadn't specifically planned it, why not let some individual imaginations come up with the reasons a financial man from a major oil company was with us.

JB and I reviewed our progress since the December meeting and answered more questions. Then, at last, Walter Byers spoke his first words to us.

Never moving in his chair, he lowered his head, peered over his glasses and chided, "Seems to me like you're looking for a hunting license. We give you a contract, and you go out hunting for money, advertisers and cable customers."

JB answered, "That's not quite right, Mr. Byers. However, we must have some sort of indication or commitment to satisfy our investors and the cable industry that we mean business."

Walter challenged, "Suppose we give you a commitment, and you go out hunting and don't come up with the money. How do we know we'll get paid?"

My turn to answer, *"You name the bank, and we'll put 50 percent of the agreed contract price in escrow on July 1"*.

The room was silent. JB stared at the floor; George stared at JB and swears he turned chalk-white; the committee members stared at each other, but Walter and I never broke eye contact.

"Well, if you can do that, it sounds pretty good to me. We'll have to think about it."

No more questions; we were free to go!

Once we reached the hotel lobby, JB recovered his voice and asked, Why did you say that? We might not even be around in July!"

"What was I supposed to say? Besides, July is a long way off, and we'll have the money by then."

George was very quiet. I knew he was still evaluating us, and I wondered if I had just given him some bad things to report.

Before we had time to really worry too much, Tom Hansen came looking for us to ask if we could come back for a meeting at Shawnee Mission next Wednesday, January 31. He said Walter wanted to talk to us at the NCAA office. Quickly, we agreed to meet at 9 a.m. next Wednesday.

Well, so much for worrying about my brash promise to escrow some money on July 1. I just hoped Walter was picking out his bank. George and I headed west to L.A., while JB returned to Philadelphia. D-day (for Disaster) was drawing near for our tiny company. It was so frustrating. The little guys from Connecticut had lots of giant balloons in the air with major national entities, and yet we couldn't collect paychecks or pay our bills! The financial sands of our company's life were running out.

That's exactly what I told Scott as I arrived at his hotel room at 2 a.m. The hour was insignificant. We had to talk! I explained all the positive news I had, and he told me about Compact Video. We ordered breakfast from room service.

A courtesy visit to Evey took up part of the next day and gave Scott an opportunity to meet the Getty V.P. We then proceeded to Compact Video.

The brass not only rolled out the red carpet, but also rolled out a model of their proposed 40-foot remote production television van. I was impressed. Scott had said they were good, and their enthusiastic, thorough presentation made a great first impression on me.

Saturday afternoon, Scott and I flew back to Connecticut. Early Monday, January 29th, Bob Chamberlain and I drove to New York City to meet again with Gene Petrillo at D'Arcy. We filled him in on our last week's activity, and he was impressed. He then startled us when he asked, "How does $1,380,000 sound for your 1/8 package?"

How does it sound? "Great!" we chorused. Bob had called Gene after our meeting last week and told him our decision about the $500,000 offer.

"We've got a lot of work to do, and you have to put your house in order, but I want you to know we're interested. Furthermore, if you have any interest from any other beer sponsors, please call me. I want that exclusive," Gene emphasized.

Not a bad start for the week! On Tuesday, JB and I met with Chuck Dolan, originator of the Home Box Office project in the '60's and now president and owner of Cablevision, a giant Long Island cable MSO. Chuck suggested we abandon our ad-supported philosophy and go all-pay. We had sought his interest as an investor. Not only was he uninterested in investing, but he just didn't think we were on the right track.

That afternoon JB and I left again for Kansas City.

Wednesday, January 31, NCAA Headquarters
Shawnee Mission, Kansas

No TV Committee this time. Walter Byers was very much in charge of the meeting attended by the NCAA's Tom Hansen and Dennis Cryder, JB and me. That's all! We spent virtually the entire day discussing possible scenarios for an arrangement. Walter was extremely enthusiastic about the potential. He and I explored all sorts of subjects including scheduling, producton, promotion, advertising, cable systems, subscriber charges and finances!

"The annual Texas Show is next week in San Antonio, Walter. It's the third largest industry show each year. If we're going to do something, that will be a great place to announce it. Is that possible?" I asked.

"It might be," Walter hinted. "We have a lot of work to do, but it's possible. Can you come back here next week on your way to the show?"

"Absolutely! I'll even bring some stationery; then, if we agree to something, we can do a press release on the spot. Is Wednesday morning good for you?"

"Yes—we'll see you then," Walter concluded.

Now, that was really positive! The crusty chief of collegiate sports was very friendly and seemed to indicate he was going to do something—we couldn't guess what—to help us at the Texas Show.

Again I flew west and JB east. He was still trolling for possible investors and would continue to do so in case Getty said no.

I met George Conner, and we reviewed everything accomplished to date. Amazingly, an awful lot had happened in just under two months, but Getty was still hesitant to make a move.

After I updated the folks at Compact Video, they volunteered to bring their model E.S.P. Network truck to the Texas Show so that I could display it during my brief, five-minute presentation on a "new program suppliers" panel.

Another Saturday cross-country hop and back in the Plainville office on Sunday, February 4. Two days catching up on Ed's travels and his work with Bristol's Redevelopment Authority; an update from Bob Chamberlain on his advertising and programming efforts; Scott talked about a young architect, G. Geoffrey Bray, he thought could design our building, and they all wanted to hear about Getty and the NCAA. Throughout January and February, the troops, Bob Chamberlain particularly, called me all over the country. I could count on the message light in my hotel room being lit wherever and whenever I arrived. I can't blame them. I was just as curious about their progress, but I was involved with the gigantic items of interest— money and programming! Needless to say, they all had every right to be curious, and I had to keep them informed.

February 6th I left for Shawnee Mission again and that night met JB at the Airport Marriot Hotel. We reviewed a few things for our morning meeting and got a good night's sleep.

Wednesday, February 7, NCAA Headquarters
Shawnee Mission, Kansas

That Walter wanted to strike a deal was clear to us immediately. First, we didn't meet at the Marriott, we met in the conference room at NCAA headquarters. Second, the taciturn czar of the TV Committee meeting room was now all smiles as he greeted us warmly. Third, as he sat down at the head of the conference table, he told me to take the seat nearest him.

As we settled in comfortably for the day's meeting, I was thinking about tomorrow's scheduled panel appearance at the annual Texas Cable Show in San Antonio. What a coup it would be to announce a potential NCAA affiliation there! With mounting enthusiasm and dwindling patience, I answered questions about countless details. Finally I blurted out, "Can we make some sort of an announcement tomorrow in San Antonio?"

"What's it worth to you?" Walter countered.

"An awful lot. We'll get exposure in the cable trades and a chance to add a lot of credibility to our story."

"Sounds to me like that's worth about $100,000," Walter smiled.

"Probably a lot more," I conceded.

"Did you bring your checkbook with you?" he continued.

"No!" It wouldn't have made any difference. It didn't have any money in it anyway, I thought to myself.

"Well, how about wiring $25,000 to us, and we'll draft up a little something for you to read." Walter was toying with JB and me.

"How about drafting up a little something for us to read, and we'll come back next week with our attorney and begin drafting a contract?" I asked.

"We might be able to do something like that. Where do you stand with Getty?"

"We expect to hear from them momentarily. They're curious about the reaction at the Texas Show and want to hear where we stand with you," I replied.

"What about that $25,000 wire?" Walter was back to money.

"What about a little something to read tomorrow, and we'll talk about deposits and escrow accounts next week when we come back?"

"O.K., let's see what we can put together," he
concluded. He must have known we didn't have
any money in the bank all along. He agreed to a
brief release confirming our discussions that said
an agreement "might" be reached soon. We
agreed to meet on Valentine's Day with
attorneys for both sides present.

The finish line was in sight with the NCAA,
but we still needed that Getty commitment.
Wednesday evening I flew to San Antonio.

Thursday, February 8
Texas Cable Show
San Antonio, Texas

Complete with the model truck, the Compact
Video people sat in the front row awaiting my
scheduled appearance on the "new program suppliers" panel. The panel was chaired by the mysterious Greg Liptak who had missed our
scheduled meeting in Austin back in December.

I was the next to last speaker. On cue, as I was
introduced, Oscar Wilson, Compact Video's
white-haired, scholarly Vice President, moved to
the stage. With tongue in cheek and a twinkle in
his eye, he parked our model truck for all the
world to see just to the left of where I was
standing.

During my brief five minutes, I outlined our
planned 24-hour, ad-supported sports network
produced with first-class equipment, such as the

model shown on stage. In the final minute
allowed me, I read the NCAA release.

Now, that was a lot for some 800 Texans and
the assembled national cable media to swallow
from a Yankee: a basic channel, 24 hours a day,
all sports, advertiser supported, and the NCAA
potential involvement! Since no one in the industry guessed how far along we were, my announce-
ments sent a shock wave through those folks
that listened. I sat down. Liptak concluded the
panel, and the assembly broke for coffee.

Never one to miss a sales opportunity, Oscar
moved quickly to pick up the model truck and
walked down the center aisle toward the exit
before anyone made a move. What a marketing
ploy! He did it so quickly and so well that I think
many in the audience thought they were supposed to wait until he passed before they left
their seats to follow him.

Oscar wasn't finished! Just outside the meeting room doors he commandeered a trash barrel,
and, using the model's packing box, created an
instant display for everyone to see as they left
the hall. He even threw down a few Compact
Video brochures and business cards and did a
brisk few minutes explaining the virtues of
E.S.P. and Compact Video.

I'll never forget one gentleman from Bartles-
ville, Oklahoma, who said to me as I left the
stage, "I don't know how you're going to do all
you said, but if you only do half of it, you'll be

the most successful service we have." How
prophetic.

I was not exactly besieged by reporters, but
the cable press did come to ask for more of the
story. Perfect! We really needed some sort of a
boost for Getty, the NCAA, D'Arcy and the
MSOs. We had been running on "smoke and
mirrors" for so long, they were getting thin.

Back to Plainville on Friday to find desperation closing in. We had no money for next week's
payroll, and JB had told Scott that K.S. Sweet
had decided to stop funding us. If something
didn't happen by the 15th—just 6 days from
now—we were out of business!

Monday, the 12th, Ed and Scott had to do a
song and dance for the Bristol Redevelopment
Authority and succeeded in getting a two-week
extension before losing our position on the land
we wanted to buy.

JB was very low. He had arranged for me to
visit Taft Broadcasting in Cincinnatti on my
way to Kansas City on the 13th, but was so
discouraged that he didn't plan to attend.

"I don't know why we're even going to meet
Byers. We can't sign a contract even if we want
to—we can't pay for it."

"Let's try Evey one more time," I suggested.

"O.K!" he reluctantly agreed. That call drove
JB even deeper into depression.

"Stu says if we insist on an answer today, it's No!' I really think we should call off the NCAA meeting and save the plane fare," JB grumbled.

"We've come this far, and we have our tickets," I said. "Let's play out the string."

"Yeah, we might as well! See you in Kansas City. Good luck with Taft."

JB's depression was easily understood. Originally, K.S. Sweet had committed to a $75,000 interim funding plan. Our last advance from them put their commitment to us well over $200,000, and JB's partners had finally said, "Whoa!"

Wednesday, February 14, NCAA Headquarters
Shawnee Mission, Kansas

Tuesday's meeting at Taft proved fruitless, and JB and I arrived for our 9:30 a.m. meeting with attorneys in tow to discuss a contract it looked like we'd never sign. Hot coffee and Danish were in plentiful supply as Walter, Tom and Dennis greeted us and introduced Dick Andrews, one of the NCAA attorneys. For our part, JB had enlisted John Bales, a Philadelphia lawyer (that produced plenty of bad jokes, as you might suspect), and we all sat down to talk contract.

Walter and I explained to the attorneys what we were trying to accomplish, and they took copious notes. We were really in gear just 90 minutes later and feeling much better about our prospects for success, when one of the NCAA secretaries interrupted to tell me I had a phone call. Expecting the worst, I excused myself and took the call in Dennis Cryder's office.

"Bill, this is George. Our strategy committee has given us the go-ahead! Mr. Evey was wondering if you could come to California later today?"

How do you calmly respond to an opening telephone salvo like that? "I'll be there," was all I could manage.

George went on, "Even though the strategy committee has recommended we proceed, you'll still have to meet a couple of people before we get final approval. However, we're better than 90 percent there, and I'm sure you'll do fine when you meet these men. Tentatively, I'd say congratulations are in order."

"George, can I say anything to the NCAA people here?" I was recovering my composure.

"You can tell them just what I told you. You'll probably have a definite answer for them by tomorrow or Friday. By the way, how's everything going in Shawnee Mission today?"

"Just great, George, great—and it'll be even better now. I'll see you at the Getty offices at 8 tomorrow morning . . . and thanks, George, for all you've done."

"Don't thank me. I think it's a great project, and Getty wouldn't have this opportunity if it weren't for you. See you in the morning."

I guess my smile gave me away as I walked back into the conference room. Walter immediately queried, "Good news?"

JB was curious, too.

"That was George Conner. Getty wants us to come directly to L.A., JB, to meet a couple of more people, but their strategy committee has approved our proposal. George said there are some details to work out, but we'll solve them."

As you can imagine, the rest of the NCAA contract discussion proceeded with a vibrant new feeling of confidence on both sides. Personally, I couldn't wait to get outside and jump in the air and click my heels. What a Valentine's Day! Ninety minutes and half a continent apart, the two "yeses" propelled us to new heights of happiness when less than 24 hours ago JB didn't even want to make the trip. Ours was definitely not a business for the faint-hearted.

We finished our preliminary contract discussions and made plans to return to the NCAA headquarters on the following Monday, February 19, for more contract work.

This time both JB and I headed west to meet with Evey and other Getty executives.

Thursday, February 15
Los Angeles, California

We met with Stu, George and attorney Max Gardner during the morning. Evey announced that he and I were leaving for the Burbank airport at noon. The man I had to meet was Harold Stuart, a member of the Getty Board of Directors and a former Tulsa TV station owner.

What Evey didn't tell me was that I was going to meet Mr. Stuart in Phoenix, Arizona. Not only meet him in Phoenix, but fly with him to Midland-Odessa, Texas, where Harold was attending the annual "Oil Hall of Fame!!" Well, why not? There's a baseball, basketball, football and hockey Hall of Fame, among others, so why not an "Oil Hall of Fame?"

We left Burbank in the Getty company jet bound for Phoenix. On board, in addition to Evey and myself, were Mr. and Mrs. John McCabe (a Getty Senior Group Vice President) and Mr. and Mrs. Harold Berg (Getty's Board Chairman). The seventh seat in the seven-passenger jet was saved for Mr. Stuart.

For me, it was all part of an unbelievable series of events rushing toward a climax sometime today, but who could guess when? Stuart, Berg, Evey and I talked about our project from Phoenix to Midland-Odessa, and, immediately upon landing, Evey directed me to one limousine with the two wives and John McCabe, while he, Berg and Stuart rode in a second limo. I had no idea that the final decision on the fate of E.S.P. was being made in that limo during the short, ten-minute ride from the airport to the hotel.

While I was registering at the Midland Hilton, Evey came into the tiny reception area and spotted me. Smiling, he came over and said, "Congratulations!"

"What?" I knew what I wanted that to mean, but held my emotions in check as he continued, "I said 'Congratulations!' You just got approved for your project. We'll work out the details back in L.A. tomorrow, but, for now, go change. Let's go to this reception and then have dinner. I'll meet you here in 45 minutes."

Wow! What a moment! I don't even remember finishing the registration process. Talk about happy! Talk about an emotional high! Talk about relief! E.S.P. was going to happen. We were really going to be funded and make some dreams come true.

While Evey calmly registered, I raced for the elevator to spread the good news. Forty of the forty-five minutes were spent on the phone. I never saw Harold Stuart other than on the plane from Phoenix to Midland-Odessa, but whatever he wanted to know, he apparently discovered and gave his blessing to our project.

It had been quite a week already, and it wasn't over yet.

Wheels up at 8 a.m. Friday morning and back to L.A. where George, JB and Max, the attorney, had been at work with Scott and Bob Ronstrom on the phone.

I called the NCAA office as soon as we landed to share the news and confirm our Monday meeting. I spoke with Dennis Cryder, who offered congratulations on behalf of the staff and expressed his own personal pleasure that we would be working together.

The afternoon was filled with details and discussions of options, cash advances, and certainly our now-overdue payroll. Evey asked JB to advance the necessary funds and assured him Getty would repay the dollars the following week, along with all other interim funds previously advanced.

JB called King of Prussia and the funds were transferred. Once again, there was joy in Plainville! I had been giving the troops a running commentary throughout the week, and the word of their paychecks being released sent them all off to a happy weekend wondering what it would be like working for Getty Oil.

I flew back to Hartford on Saturday. I was scheduled to fulfill a long-standing commitment as on-air talent for a two-hour gymnastics special on PBS on Sunday, February 18. JB stayed in L.A.

As soon as the telecast ended, I raced to Bradley Field for a late flight to Kansas City. Our meeting at the NCAA was scheduled for 9 a.m. and would last all day. More contract revisions and fine-tuning.

Off to L.A. early Tuesday, February 20 for the actual contract signing with Getty.

Wednesday, February 21
Los Angeles, California

The usually accommodating Mr. Evey was missing. Today's Mr. Evey was a hard-nosed, ruthless businessman who knew he was in the driver's seat and simply wrung every advantage he could out of our hides to the benefit of Getty. He knew we'd sink without Getty, and so did we. We had little choice but to agree to his demands.

Without getting into the details, Getty basically bought an option on February 22, 1979, by agreeing to fund us until they decided to exercise that option or abandon the project. From our point of view, they were bailing us out and paying off K.S. Sweet's interim loan to the E.S.P. Network. As long as our projections held, they would keep funding us. Evey had decided to send George Conner to Connecticut for "a few months" to oversee the funds being advanced and to do continuing research.

With these details set, Getty wired some funds to Bob Ronstrom in Plainville for deposit to our account, and I signed an E.S.P. Network check repaying K.S. Sweet in full for the funds they had advanced, along with a small fee for their services.

It had been oh, so close to disaster, but we were, temporarily at least, out of the woods. I was exhausted. In the last forty-five days, I had flown to Kansas City for eight meetings and Los Angeles six times, with side trips to San Antonio,

Cincinnatti, Washington D.C., Midland-Odessa, and New York City. But, we had our funding; we had our NCAA agreement and we had our first major advertiser. Bring on the Getty team! We were set to roar into spring, and George Conner would be on hand to help us in just a few days.

Chapter 7

Getty's Option Months

Friday, February 23, 1979
Los Angeles, California

The *Wall Street Journal* (WSJ) carried a brief story about Getty's entry into the cable business. Following Thursday's signing, Evey had invited everyone to the Wilshire Country Club, and while there, I took a call from a WSJ reporter. The story was brief, factual and made no claim for a grandiose future. Quite simply, it reported that Getty had acquired an option to purchase 85% of the E.S.P. network in exchange for interim funding. Nothing fancy—just a big company with money taking advantage of an opportunity presented by a small company with no money. However, the WSJ article got the E.S.P. Network press bandwagon under way. From this modest beginning, it turned into a juggernaut. As spring turned to summer, *Sports Illustrated*, the *Sporting News*, *Business*

Week, the *New York Times*, *Newsweek* and countless other publications fueled the fires of excitement for us and America's sports junkies.

Before I get too far ahead of myself, I should point out that, during these frantic mid-February days, there were the usual ongoing projects in Plainville. The Bristol Redevelopment Authority finally gave us "tentative developer" status which allowed us to hire Geoff Bray as our architect and Dale C. Eckert Construction Company of Riverside, California. We planned to break ground just as soon as Mother Nature allowed.

The UConn package was moving along. We originated our first women's event—Harvard at UConn Ladies' Basketball—on February 6th. Now funded, we looked forward to making significant strides in cable MSO presentations and advertising sales. We were eager to have George Conner arrive and start our next phase of development.

The two agreements with the NCAA and Getty gave us a tremendous boost in credibility and respectability. Merely being associated with those prestigious names took us out of the "it'll never happen" stage to the "I think they're serious" stage as far as the cable industry was concerned.

We still had some loose ends to tie up with Evey, such as employment contracts for Scott and me (that loose end never did get tied up, as you'll see later) along with several procedural matters. Evey said we would work through George, and once George arrived in Connecticut, things should go pretty smoothly.

On that note, I flew back to Connecticut. JB had been paid off on the 22nd, and Evey made it crystal-clear that K.S. Sweet Associates' obligation had been fulfilled. Further, their services were no longer needed or even welcome. With more than a little emotion, JB and I said good-bye, and he went on his way. He and I had been through some extremely difficult days. I admired his spirit, respected his advice and valued his friendship. As I considered his contributions from September to February, I felt more than a little sad that he wouldn't be along with us for all of the excitement just ahead.

Tuesday, February 27
Kansas City, Missouri

Just a quick stop here today to meet with Cecil Coleman (the new TV Committee chairman), Walter Byers and Tom Hansen to review the contract draft and take a copy with me to L.A. for Thursday's meeting with Stu Evey.

Thursday, March 1
Los Angeles, California

A different Stu Evey welcomed me to Getty's 18th floor executive inner sanctum today. This Stu Evey was television's newest executive. He was no longer a mere oil company vice president. He had plans! Oh, did he have plans. The first one was to replace me with "someone who knows what he is doing." What he said was that he wanted to begin a search for a major network executive who could run the day-to-day business. He wanted someone with contacts in the sports world—"a heavy hitter!" Stu had already picked out the man to do the search, and we were scheduled to fly to Palm Desert Saturday morning to meet him.

Saturday, March 3
Palm Desert, California

It took us a few moments to find him, but we finally met in the golf club coffee shop.

"Bill, say hello to Ed Hookstratten," Evey began. E. Gregory Hookstratten was and still is agent extraordinaire. Among his clients at the time: Phyllis George, Tom Snyder, Tom Brokaw, Al Michaels and Dick Vermeil.

"What are you doing with this bandit?" Ed laughed as we shook hands.

"We're just beginning to put together a sports network for cable, and he says you're the man to help us."

"Of course I am! That's why he brought you here. He wants to protect his investment, so we've got to get the right people to do the job. What do you need?"

Evey smiled at Ed's barbs and then got semi-serious. "Bill's plan calls for a nationally known announcer. We're also interested in identifying a major network executive to run the operation."

We traded banter for a few more minutes. Then Ed concluded, "I can get the job done for you, but I'm expensive."

"We'll talk about that in L.A.," Evey chuckled.

"Sure, we'll talk about it in L.A., but you'll pay my fees because you know I'll deliver. Now I'm going to play golf—get out of here. Good to meet you, Bill, see you in L.A. Be careful of this guy," he said, slapping Evey on the back.

On that note, we flew directly to Los Angeles International for my connection with a flight to Hartford. During the cross-country flight, I sketched out some drafts of ideas for promotional material and made a note to ask Guy Wilson, our printer, for some suggestions on a new logo. Evey wasn't the only one with plans.

I was tired, yet eager to get back because George Conner was due in the office first thing Monday morning.

Monday, March 5
Plainville, Connecticut

Everyone arrived early to meet and greet "the Getty man," George Conner. Nine o'clock, ten o'clock, then finally 11 a.m. and still no sign of George or any word as to his whereabouts. It was

too early to call the West Coast to see if he had
changed his plans, so we just waited.

A little after eleven a.m., he arrived, but I'll let
him pick up the story at this point:

"I will never forget my first day in
Connecticut:

"Scene: front desk at the Holiday Inn.

"Desk clerk: 'Mr. Conner, what does this note
mean?'

"G.C.: 'I don't know, but if you'll read it to me,
I might be able to help.'

"Desk clerk (obviously a little nervous): 'It
says you may be driving a stolen car!'

"Someone had stolen the front license plate
from the Hertz rental car I was driving and used
it while committing an armed robbery less than a
block away. With an 'all points bulletin' out for
my car, I drove the back roads to Bradley
International Airport to trade it for a car that
would attract less interest from Connecticut
lawmen.

"In my new rental car I arrived at the office to
find that I had no place to park. The three
parking spaces for nine employees didn't quite
work. At that moment, I realized life would not
be easy during my adventure with this fast-
growing and uncertain industry."

It's fair to say George wasn't too productive
his first day in Connecticut. He had to tell his
"stolen car" story, meet everyone, and get settled in his new office. That in itself was quite a

task because he had to share a 10' x 12' room with Bob Ronstrom, three file cabinets, and some miscellaneous storage. Although he didn't say anything, he must have longed for his sump- tuous Getty quarters and his Marina del Rey apartment.

We spent the first part of the week bringing George up to speed on various aspects of our burgeoning business. Thursday, I once again flew to Kansas City.

Friday, March 9, NCAA Headquarters Shawnee Mission, Kansas

Contract signing time! Just two days short of five months since being introduced to the E.S.P. Network concept, the NCAA prepared to sign a two-year agreement. To say this was an exciting day for me personally would be a significant understatement. However, it was also a pioneer- ing day for the NCAA as it once again led its member institutions into unexplored television territory. Further, the signing represented still another step along the road of credibility for E.S.P., in particular, and the cable industry in general.

Amazingly, the actual signing was something of an anticlimax to the February 14th verbal agreement. The intervening days had been filled with meetings, lawyers, phone calls and explana- tions. The signing meeting itself was actually fairly brief and very relaxed. Walter Byers inquired about progress with the MSOs and financing and then, without much ceremony, asked the attorneys, "How many of these do you want signed? Is half a dozen enough?"

Dick Andrews, the NCAA attorney who drafted the agreement, nodded and Walter began signing and passing the documents to me for my signature.

As I signed, I couldn't help but think of that first meeting at the very same table just five months earlier. Despite the cautioning comments from Tom Hansen and Dennis Cryder in October about how slowly the NCAA worked on new projects such as E.S.P., the deal was done! A lot of hard work and cooperation on both sides made it happen.

The agreement (actually dated March 1, 1979) held not only the practical terms of performance required of both parties, but was an historic document in that it represented the NCAA's first venture into satellite technology and cable television.

AGREEMENT

Agreement dated as of this 1st day of March, 1979, between
THE NATIONAL COLLEGIATE ATHLETIC ASSOCIATION, an unincorporated association with executive offices at U. S. Highway 50, Nall Avenue, Shawnee
Mission, Kansas 66222 (hereinafter called "the NCAA"), and THE ENTER-
TAINMENT AND SPORTS PROGRAMMING NETWORK, INC., a Connecticut corporation
with executive offices at 319 Cooke Street, Plainville, Connecticut
06062 (hereinafter called "ESPN").

WITNESSETH:

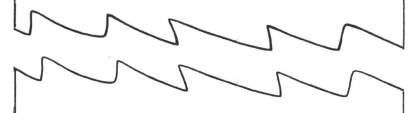

44.   Successors. This Agreement shall be binding upon the successors
and assigns of the NCAA and ESPN.

IN WITNESS WHEREOF, the parties hereto have executed this Agreement
as of the day and year first above written above.

                              THE NATIONAL COLLEGIATE ATHLETIC
                                 ASSOCIATION

                              By: _____
                                    Executive Director

                              THE ENTERTAINMENT AND SPORTS PROGRAMMING
                              NETWORK, INC.

                              By: _____
                                    President

ATTEST:

_____
Secretary

March 12-16

Off to Denver to meet Bob Seidenglanz, President of Compact Video, and Dale Eckert, President of Dale C. Eckert Corporation, to review studio plans and then returned to Kansas City on Tuesday for more NCAA conversation. I was looking forward to getting all this behind me so I could get back to Plainville for a scheduled Friday meeting with Scientific Atlanta's Ed Pietras. Ed had all the specs for our uplink, and I was anxious to insure that all went well between him and George. It did, and we placed our order—just under a half-million dollars—and looked forward to installation in August.

Saturday, March 17
Columbus, Ohio

I flew to Columbus to attend our first cable trade show since Texas. While we were excited and Getty was enthused, the attendees at the Ohio Show barely took note of E.S.P. Network.

Undaunted, I flew to Denver to renew our MSO conversations and hopefully get some letters of intent to take with me to L.A. later in the week.

Wednesday, March 21
Denver, Colorado

A busy line-up started with a visit to Gene Schneider at United Cable.

"Congratulations, Bill—landing the NCAA and Getty is quite a coup."

"Thanks, Gene, but we've still got an awful lot of work to do. Now we have to get some subscribers."

"How can we help? Do you have any contracts yet? Are you ready to sign people?"

I was smiling inwardly at Gene's enthusiasm. He had said he wanted to be our first MSO when we spoke back in December, and now it sure sounded to me like he was ready to sign. I didn't have any contracts, but I did ask, "Gene, can you draft a letter of intent that says United will carry our service when we launch?"

"Certainly! By the way, do you still plan to launch the service in the fall?"

This had been a serious topic of conversation, not only for all of us in Plainville, but with the NCAA and Getty as well. When we had no money, it was tough to sound convincing about launching a new cable service on a specific date. However, as soon as Getty was assured, we made the decision to start our new service at 7 p.m. on Friday, September 7, 1979.

To digress for just a second, let me explain why the launch time we chose was so specific. Many cable networks had come and gone in the past. Ad hoc nets, bicycle nets, you name it. Many had given a tentative launch date to the industry and then not delivered. Having been burned many times in the past, the cable industry was skeptical of target dates. We were determined to deliver our first telecast as advertised. It turned out to be quite a task, but more about that later. Now back to Gene Schneider.

"Gene, we'll launch at 7 p.m. Eastern Daylight Time, Friday, September 7. A commitment such as yours will help make that possible."

"Well, count us in. Put your contracts in order and let's get them signed," Gene concluded.

"One other thing," I said, "I'd like your permission to do a press release saying we've reached an agreement and that United is our first customer."

"That's fine! Draft it, have someone read it to me, and get it out as soon as you can," he answered.

I left United and visited Graham Moore at TCI, Susan Frost at Cablecom and Tom Johnson at Daniels. No reception mirrored the enthusiasm of Gene Schneider's at United, but all were interested, and Tom wasn't chuckling any more. Again the Getty and NCAA credibility factor helped earn a serious reception for what I had to say.

Back in Plainville, Bob Ronstrom and Scott were getting ready for the Bristol Redevelopment Authority meeting. We had already been given permission to do preliminary site work, but tonight's meeting promised action on being named "the developer," which would allow us to go full speed ahead. As it turned out, the meeting proved routine, and the Authority authorized us to proceed.

Actually, things settled into a pretty normal (for us) routine for the next couple of weeks. There was a flurry of trips to L.A., San Francisco, Denver, Atlanta, New York and Boston, but the Getty/NCAA magic was working wonders. Advertising agencies returned our phone calls as did cable industry heavyweights. We continued to draw more and more attention from both the national and cable industry press. Our pursuit of MSOs and advertisers continued, as did our UConn coverage. We managed an early morning meeting the first week of April with Ed Hookstratten during one visit to L.A., in which he suggested that Jim Simpson, NBC's popular veteran sportscaster, might be available if we were interested. He also trotted out Chet Simmons' name as a possible chief operating officer. Chet had been president of NBC Sports since 1977 and certainly had the credentials.

By this time, we were so confident of the E.S.P. Network concept that it never occurred to us that anyone we approached would even hesitate if we offered them an employment opportunity. We found out later it wasn't quite that easy.

April 14-15, Easter Weekend
Monte Carlo Grand Prix

Our next big programming project was the World Cup Tennis Tournament, the Grand Prix from Monte Carlo, scheduled Easter weekend. From our point of view, it might better have been called the E.S.P. Circus from Monte Carlo.

We were still woefully thin on people, but several of our 15-man staff put on different hats and produced E.S.P. Network's very first international event. Here's how it worked:

1. The time difference worked in our favor since Monte Carlo is several hours ahead of U.S. time zones. Combined with the daylight play at the tournament, this allowed us to fly the video tapes to the U.S. for prime time viewing.

2. Bob Chamberlain flew to Monte Carlo to coordinate the BBC feed which would incorporate E.S.P.

3. Scott and long-time friend Bill MacDade flew to Paris to pick up the completed tapes and return with them to New York's Kennedy Airport (Bill to fly back with Saturday's tapes; Scott with Sunday's).

4. Peter Fox stationed himself at Customs at Kennedy to receive tapes of the tournament and rush them to Manhattan Cable.

5. Manhattan Cable in New York City cooperated and agreed to let us use their

facility to feed RCA's Vernon Valley uplink to transponder 7.

6. Dennis Randall, our new Public Relations Director, Lou Palmer and all the rest of us got on the phones to line up as many subscribers as possible.

Well, with a flaky set-up like that you probably think our odds of success were slim. You're right—they were! Our telephone campaign, though, produced nearly 2 million potential subscriber homes, so we had to deliver.

Amazingly, everything came off with a minimum of difficulty. Bob Chamberlain even got the BBC to tape a special open and close just for us and Bill MacDade brought that back with the tapes of the Saturday matches.

You might be interested to know that in Europe at a tournament such as this one there is only one video feed to a central point, Paris, in this case, and several audio feeds. In other words, Scott, standing in the control room in Paris, watched the tennis tournament, but heard not only the BBC English version, but also the French, German, Spanish, et al, audio feeds destined for other European countries. Just one more seemingly confused exercise handled with dispatch by our "crisis control experts."

When all was said and done, we even surprised ourselves. George Conner was impressed, and so were quite a few cable operators. We were really eager to get to the National Cable Television

Association (NCTA) show in Las Vegas in May. We couldn't wait to see what kind of a reaction there would be to our all-sports, 24 hour concept.

With Monte Carlo behind us, it was business as usual in Bristol. The first bite of the bulldozer's blade on our newly acquired land was taken in late March, and during these first few weeks of April, it seemed to us that all the construction crews were accomplishing was moving piles of earth from place to place. It was impossible to imagine that in five and a half months a building would even be standing, much less a building filled with highly sophisticated television equipment producing a live picture. As a matter of fact, we discovered that a huge majority of people who saw the construction progress through spring and into summer were skeptics. They thought we were a bit wacky to talk about a cable network feeding sports all day long in the first place, but they were absolutely convinced we knew nothing of the impossible task of building a home for that network in less than six months. They were probably right, but we didn't know any better. We had a deadline to meet.

Monday, April 16
Norfolk, Virginia

Unable to rest on our Monte Carlo tennis laurels, Ron Newman, Affiliate Relations Manager, and I flew to Norfolk, Virginia, on Easter

Monday to meet with Dick Roberts and Gordon Herring of Telecable. One more flight; one more MSO visit; one more commitment to our network! This was getting easier by the day because of the credibility added to our network by both Getty's option and the NCAA contract. E.S.P. Network was rapidly becoming the "favored new network" among MSOs because, with each passing day, we were more believable. All of this is not to say that potential affiliates immediately lined up to sign contracts. However, they all knew about us and were eager to learn all about our programming and pricing.

MSO activity continued to go well. Cox Communications Vice President, Ernie Olson, committed to us in April. Our list was growing. The week after our tennis extravaganza, Gulf Coast Cable, Houston, Texas signed on. I mention Gulf Coast because they gave us our first check. Our contract called for a substantial discount for early payment when signing the contract, and system General Manager Dick Barron, a former advertising executive I had known in the mid-'60's, wanted that discount.

During this period, we hired two affiliate relations representatives to work with Newman. We also added more secretarial and accounting help. Finally, the network was beginning to look and act like a real business.

On the West Coast, Compact Video answered countless questions for Getty's Evey about our remote facilities and purchased the first of two 40-foot vans that would ultimately form the backbone of the ESPN remote fleet. Evey was really anxious to be involved in show business and was determined to be the man in charge. He constantly reminded us that he could shut off the dollar faucet with a snap of his fingers.

May, 1979

As the calendar turned to May, an already hectic pace quickened in anticipation of the National Cable Television Association (NCTA) national show in Las Vegas. The show opened on May 20th, and we had to design, construct and ship an exhibit to the Las Vegas Convention Center by May 10th. Although our tiny staff was not growing, the tasks to be performed by that staff certainly were.

Talks continued with the NCAA and other potential programmers, Getty, MSOs, Compact Video, Eckert Construction, and now with our exhibit designers. At times, it felt as if we were awake around the clock. We traveled on overnight flights to arrive for morning meetings. We met at 7:00 am or 11:00 pm ... whatever it took to get the various jobs done.

Two significant meetings need to be mentioned. First, at a routine update for Getty's strategy committee, we received an interesting insight into just how tiny a part we played in the overall Getty scheme of things. As questions and answers dragged on, John McCabe, Senior Group Vice President and an oil industry veteran who worked his way up the corporate ladder from the oil fields, abruptly brought the meeting to an end. "Why are we taking so long to make up our minds? Far as I'm concerned, this isn't even as costly as drilling a dry hole, and we drill lots of those. Let's get on with it!"

We also formalized our Budweiser commitment with a full-blown presentation at the Anheuser-Busch brewery in St. Louis. A-B's Mike Roarty, Vice President/Marketing, and D'Arcy's Gene Petrillo arranged for us to explain E.S.P. to key people so that they could begin to include us in their advertising plans for our launch in September. This meeting put the finishing touch to our $1,380,000 contract and, with Budweiser, we proudly announced to the world the largest single advertising contract ever signed in the cable industry. Not bad, for a network that wasn't even going on the air 'til September. Not bad at all!!

All the while, construction continued at a seemingly leisurely pace in Bristol, but we knew that it was progressing just as fast as it could. After all, how fast can concrete harden? Footings and foundations had to be in place before the steel arrived. As we left for Las Vegas, the E.S.P. Network Broadcast Center was still just a hole in the ground with ribbons of concrete stretching in various directions.

A stopover in Tempe, Arizona, was part of my itinerary en route to Las Vegas. The PAC-10 Athletic Directors were meeting. We were invited to explain to the A.D.'s how the recently signed NCAA contract would work and how much money each university could expect in rights fees. You must understand that the NCAA controls no regular season varsity events. The rights belong to the home team in all cases. In 1978, many schools were just beginning to explore the potential of cable to produce dollars and, as a result of the E.S.P./NCAA agreement, the process had been accelerated in most conferences. Our presentation at the Tempe meeting was really just informational for both sides. After asking lots of questions and learning quite a bit about cable, the A.D.'s left us with the impression that they weren't really too interested in regular-season participation with us. The NCAA guaranteed championship events, but we needed the cooperation of all the major conferences to present geographically balanced programming to our viewers. While discouraged at the time by the disquieting PAC-10 derailment of our E.S.P. Network Express, performance was on our side, and the conference was included in our schedule by the time we went on the air in September.

Sunday, May 20
Las Vegas, Nevada

Bob Ronstrom, Bob Bray and one secretary were the only people not making the trip to Las Vegas. We even recruited wives, girlfriends and relatives to help assemble information packets and man our tiny hospitality suite. If Monte Carlo was an E.S.P. circus, Las Vegas was an extravaganza. With few people and only 200 square feet of display space (10' by 20') at the rear of the exhibit hall, we drew crowds that even the biggest optimist could not have anticipated. Everyone had a program, owned rights to an event, wanted either to sell advertising or go to work for us. We were overwhelmed! Evey and George Conner were present, of course, and continued their "investigation and research." Remember, we were still operating under that option . . . the final Getty commitment had not yet been made.

Well, the hubbub on the convention floor and the electric feeling of success that glowed from our tiny exhibit space apparently convinced Evey that it was time to move on that option. He left the convention a day early and returned to Los Angeles. George asked me on Wednesday, the 23rd, to make arrangements to fly to L.A. and meet with Evey on the 25th. More on that shortly.

Before I get too far ahead of myself again, let me tell you a little bit about the NCTA National

Show debut for E.S.P. The convention floor was continuous activity. Potential programmers, customers, employees, salesmen and the curious all seemed to be demanding our attention at the same time. However, the Hospitality Suite was the place to be to meet and talk to people about business . . . like the Ladies' Championship Wrist Wrestling promoter who arrived the first night.

The promoter, who, mercifully, shall remain nameless, was about 5'4" tall and had with him the "current Ladies" World Wrist Wrestling champion." She was about eight inches taller than he, and, as far as I was concerned, could have the championship of anything she wanted. This was one big, strong woman! Well, about 6 or 6:30 p.m., the promoter, realizing he wasn't being taken very seriously, decided to issue challenges to anyone in the suite to test his champion. Naturally, there were no takers at 6:30 or 7:30 or even at 9:00 p.m. However, by 3 a.m., one prominent gentleman felt much stronger than he had earlier in the evening and accepted the challenge. The bar was cleared, and the contest began. The promoter was to referee, and his protegee won the first try in about two seconds. Subsequent tries were even quicker. Even Ben Davidson, in a popular beer commercial, takes nearly 30 seconds to win.

On the serious side, we did have countless cable operators and MSOs come to the suite to discuss potential contracts with us. We even had an advertising agency representative or two among our guests.

We also had Lady Luck visit us. We discovered she was smiling on the Rasmussens when my son, Glenn, appeared at the suite early Monday evening with an ice bucket in his hand and announced that he had "won some quarters." It seems he was walking through the casino at the Las Vegas Hilton and had one quarter in his pocket. He promptly played a Keno machine. The "some quarters" that came tumbling out as he won totaled $200.00! Not bad for one quarter invested, and a good omen for things to come for E.S.P. With that kind of luck following him around, we decided we needed him near the E.S.P. project all the time. When he returned to Connecticut, Glenn promptly began work at the Bristol building site for Dale Eckert.

Friday, May 25
Los Angeles, California

Meeting with Evey in the morning was almost an anticlimax to the enthusiastic and exciting convention just completed. He simply announced that Getty planned to exercise their option on June 1 and he had a letter for me to sign acknowledging that exercise. Upon exercising the option, Getty owned 85% of E.S.P., and the original shareholders were diluted by that amount. (The specifics are far more complicated, but essentially this was the net result). All of this was done in about 10 minutes. Getty provided funding in exchange for the option. It now merely transferred some dollars back to me to repay advances made to the company several months earlier by Scott and me, and the deal was done. There were no big dollars exchanged, no pictures for the press, no elation. Realistically, the dreamers, "us little guys from Connecticut," had just lost our company. Oh, I got a pay raise and was earning a six-figure salary for the first time in my life, and that was certainly cause for joy. But giving up E.S.P. did not set well. Unfortunately, we had no choice. Had Getty pulled the financial plug at that point, all the hard work and success we had enjoyed would have gone for naught.

Getty didn't pull the plug. In his new role, Evey was even more enamoured of the TV world, but that was working in E.S.P.'s favor. Maybe we didn't control the company any more. But no one knew where the network was going better than we did, and we were going to launch on September 7! There was work to do, a business to build, people to hire and a facility to complete. On paper, Getty owned it, but we quickly discovered that to the cable world and the media, it was Getty's money and our idea. Life wasn't so bad, after all, as we began the stretch run toward September 7th.

Chapter 8

Here Come the Heavyweights

June, 1979

The exercise of the Getty option spurred activity on all fronts. As Getty put its full resources behind the project, we discovered we had considerable internal housekeeping to do. Forms, procedures and plans needed to be formalized and recorded properly, not just talked about and scribbled on a few scraps of paper. Much to my frustration, most of the month was spent this way. I knew we had to conform, but it seemed to me that we were slowing our efforts to launch our new service September 7th.

Now that Getty was totally committed, Evey launched his "heavy hitter" search in earnest. He wanted a big name heading the operation, not some little guy from Connecticut. Ed Hookstratten specifically identified Chester R. (Chet) Simmons, President of NBC Sports, and Jim Simpson, popular NBC play-by-play veteran, as the two national figures to be pursued. Bob Wussler, former President of CBS, was briefly considered, but he ultimately moved to Ted Turner's Superstation as the Chief Operating Officer.

The recruiting of Simmons began with a series of phone calls: Ed to Chet; Chet to me; me to Stu; Stu to Chet; Stu to me; etc. Chet was still President of NBC Sports and, for obvious reasons, preferred that our conversations be kept very quiet. This was especially appropriate since just a couple of months prior to our discussion, Chet had publicly stated that "the E.S.P. total sports idea wasn't going to succeed." Admittedly, when he made that statement, he knew nothing of the cable business and was, as they say, "shooting from the hip" with his negative comments.

With Getty money behind the negotiations, Chet wasn't nearly as negative or hesitant about the cable business as he had been just weeks earlier. Getty money, coupled with the fact that his NBC contract was up for renewal, made Chet an eager listener to the E.S.P. proposition.

Friday, July 6
Bristol, Connecticut

Following the preliminary telephone sparring, I invited Chet to Bristol to see the construction progress and answer more of his questions about the cable world. To maintain the confidentiality and anonymity upon which Chet insisted, I met him and his wife at a shopping mall McDonald's. After assuring him there was no one at the site, we drove to the partially completed Broadcast Center.

The steel work had been topped off with the traditional tree being hoisted into place on July 3, and now, standing in what would ultimately be the reception area (but now was just hard-packed mud) and looking skyward through the steel beams, Chet asked: "When are you planning to go on the air?"

"September 7."

"You'll never make it!"

"We think we will," I answered. "The equipment has been ordered; Scientific Atlanta will install our uplinks early next month, and we've told both Getty and the cable industry that we'll launch on September 7."

"I'll give you credit for optimism, but I honestly don't see how you'll do it," he concluded.

Wednesday, July 11
Los Angeles, California

I flew back to the West Coast on Monday, July 9, for continued meetings with Getty. This time around, I was confronted with the Human Resources Department. This group was charged with the responsibility of evaluating people, positions and compensation for the corporation. We obviously had to get acquainted. I had to learn their systems and restrictions, and they had to learn the television business. I found it terribly constricting to have positions placed on a grid determined by job title, experience and other intangible "rating points" to discover how much an employee should be paid. They found the exaggerated salaries paid in the television industry appalling. Even more disturbing to the Human Resources folks was the wide range of salary within the same job categories, i.e., announcers, $15,000-$200,000-plus annually. That kind of range just didn't fit in the oil corporation's grid.

A lot of hard work at educating and analyzing the problems went into three days of discussions. We all came away from the meetings with a much better understanding of the difficulties we faced. To the credit of the Human Resources Department, they adapted a lot more easily to understanding the TV compensation mentality than I did to the suffocating corporate procedures.

The highlight of the day, following my last session at Getty, was a visit to Compact Video in Burbank. Our remote vans were progressing, but the real reason for my visit to Compact was to meet a photographer from *Sports Illustrated*. *SI* writer William Oscar Johnson was preparing a story on us for the magazine's TV-radio page, and he wanted a picture of me with one of our remote trucks. Since the trucks weren't far enough along for photos, we trotted out the same model Oscar Wilson displayed in San Antonio in February and got our photo . . . even staged it in front of an earth station for greater impact. Just how much impact I never imagined. I'll tell you about that shortly.

Thursday, July 12
Shawnee Mission, Kansas

Back at NCAA headquarters after the picture-taking at Compact Video, I met Jon Foley, E.S.P. Program Director. The chore for the day was a fun one. Tom Hansen, Dennis Cryder and Jim Shaffer from the NCAA staff, along with Jon and I, were scheduled to take a first pass at assembling a fall football schedule. With launch less than two months away, we had to begin to get a handle on what was available and where. We also had to learn the ground rules.

ABC had an exclusive football contract with the NCAA so that we actually had to construct some new ground rules in some cases. For example, ABC for years had been notifying the NCAA on Monday of each week which games they planned to televise on Saturday. All of that was fine, but now we were in the picture, and ABC had to make their decision by a reasonable time so that we could select our games. ABC's problem was an easy one. Whichever teams they chose were certain to accept because of the huge amounts of money involved. When it was our turn, we had no guarantee of anyone accepting because we were only planning to pay $2,750 and the telecast had to be tape-delayed to conform to our contract. A lot of schools just weren't interested for that amount of money, so we had to schedule many stand-by games each week.

Our visit had a double purpose since the TV Committee was meeting on Friday, the 13th, in Jackson Hole, Wyoming. I mention this because while the scheduling work and the TV Committee were important, they were really much less pressurized than all of our earlier meetings. The trip from Kansas City to Jackson Hole is significant, however. After a couple of Bloody Marys, some creative thinking by Jon and me produced a wide variety of necessary promotional items for us. Jon was charged with ordering everything upon his return to Connecticut.

Not even our corporate name, the E.S.P. Network, escaped our brainstorming. After all, we had funding from a major oil company, advertising from a major sports advertiser, excellent trade and consumer media coverage and contracts for service with several major MSOs. E.S.P. just didn't have the ring it had when we incorporated. We needed something better for identification and promotional purposes. First, we eliminated the word "Network" and decided to use a four-letter acronym. Who ever decreed that networks had to identify themselves with only three letters?

While playing with ideas, we added "-TV" to the letters, put an elliptical circle around "ESPN-TV" and tried the circle without the "-TV." Eventually we abandoned our "logo design discussion" and decided to give the ESPN logo project to our printer, Guy Wilson, when we got back to Connecticut. Once he got his hands on our idea, he dropped the "-TV", selected new type, added the elliptical circle to stay, and the logo you recognize today in print and on the TV screen was born. It was particularly appropriate that all of this should be decided on Friday, July 13, 1979, since our company had been incorporated exactly 52 weeks earlier, on Friday, July 14, 1978.

Saturday, July 14
Jackson Hole, Wyoming

The morning NCAA TV Committee meeting in Jackson Hole was uneventful. It was merely a progress report with both Jon and me answering questions for the Committee members. By now, we knew most of the Committee pretty well, and they invited us to stay on for an informal cocktail party that evening and to join in a round of golf on Sunday.

The cocktail party was enlightening. Our host was George McCarty, Athletic Director at the University of Wyoming. A friendly atmosphere prevailed, and, naturally, there was a lot of talk about our planned launch on September 7. There was also a lot of good-natured fun highlighted by a "sobriety experiment" conducted on some ground squirrels on the back patio of the lodge where the party was held.

The "experiment" consisted of filling ashtrays with just a little gin, bourbon, vodka, regular beer and light beer, and lining them up where the little animals could reach them. The "monitors" of this fun experiment were highly competent and very proper in maintaining strict control on the test. Obviously, they were all extremely qualified gentlemen, but they were all qualified in football matters, not laboratory testing. Darrell Royal, Eddie Crowder, Cecil Coleman, Davey Nelson, Andy Mooradien, Tom Hansen and host George McCarty, really let their hair down, so to speak, to the obvious delight of themselves and everyone at the party.

At breakfast on Sunday, prior to our golf outing, I gained more insight into the workings of the TV Committee on the ESPN project. Seated at a table with Crowder, McCarty, Royal and Wiles Halleck of the PAC-10, I discovered that Coach Royal had broken the impasse in committee back in January.

"Bill, did you know Darrell is the man who made things happen for you?" asked Crowder. Royal, the taciturn Texan, had never spoken a word during any of our appearances before the Committee.

"No, I didn't."

"Well, remember back in January when you fellas came to Kansas City?" I nodded. "After you left, he's the man who said, 'Let's either do it or not do it, but let's stop talking about it.' And that got us all moving," Crowder continued. "He's the man you can thank for saving us all a lot of time and getting an agreement with us much faster than anyone ever has before."

How about that! The two silent men, Darrell Royal of the TV Committee, and Walter Byers, Executive Director, who rarely spoke in formal meeting sessions, had made the ESPN/NCAA contract come to life. I'll forever appreciate the confidence they had in me personally and in ESPN.

The golf Sunday was planned as a relaxing break, and it was, after we got started. I had a momentary qualm when I was paired with Jim Spence, Vice President, ABC Sports, but quickly relaxed as Jim gave me three ABC golf balls and said, "Let's not talk business and have a good round."

We didn't talk much business at all, and we even played pretty well. I did find out that in Wyoming all putts are put into the hole—no "gimmes." A strong 3 iron on one of the holes left me about 6 inches from the flag for a birdie. Jim encouraged our playing partners to give me the putt, but George McCarty, our host, answered, "We don't give birdies in Wyoming. Putt!" We all had a good laugh, and I even made the putt for my only birdie of the day.

Friday, July 20
JFK International Airport, New York

A week full of phone calls to, from and about Chet Simmons culminated at JFK about 9:30 pm. Evey decided it was time to meet Chet face to face and talk seriously about Chet's moving from NBC to ESPN. One problem, though: Chet was also worrying about his upcoming NBC contract renewal date and didn't want anyone to know he was even talking to us. So I agreed to one more "red-eye" flight, this time from JFK to Los Angeles. The plan was for me to talk to Chet, answer his questions en route, and then, on Saturday, Chet and Stu could get acquainted. A decision on Chet's employment would be reached some time before the end of July.

All appeared to be going well as I checked into the TWA Ambassador Club at JFK. Chet had not arrived, but I was paged by him moments later. As we shook hands at the front desk, I noticed he was extremely nervous. He explained, "I hope there's no one on this flight that recognizes me." His concern was genuine. We had had many phone conversations since our first meeting in Bristol, but he was a long way from committing to ESPN, and he didn't want to jeopardize his NBC position.

We stayed in the Ambassador Club until just before flight time, then moved to the gate area. We actually moved into the gate area adjacent to the Los Angeles gate, again to avoid being seen. Chet chain-smoked and paced. I got the distinct feeling that he wasn't even certain he wanted to make this flight.

We waited until everyone had boarded, and, finally, he agreed to board. He hadn't seen anyone he knew and relaxed a little. He stubbed out his latest cigarette. We quickly headed for the jetway and the waiting ticket attendant. Just as we got to the entrance, a voice called out, "Hey, Chet!"

By now, Chet had me nervous, too, and we both looked startled as he turned to greet John Brodie, former San Francisco 49'er quarterback, and Merlin Olsen, former Los Angeles Ram great, both of whom worked for Chet on NBC's coverage of the American Football Conference. So much for anonymity ... so much for any meaningful discussion en route to California!

"I didn't know you were going to L.A.," Brodie greeted Chet.

"What do you have going out there?" Olsen asked.

"Say hello to Bill Rasmussen," Chet answered. That was easy! I knew who Brodie and Olsen were, but they didn't know me, so Chet was safe for the moment since he didn't say I was with ESPN. That would have raised some questions.

Chet continued, "I've got some Olympic things to attend to." NBC had the rights to the 1980 Olympics in Moscow (which the U.S. ultimately boycotted), and the answer seemed to satisfy his two announcers.

The flight was actually uneventful. We talked a lot of football and television, but no ESPN. I got to bed about 4:00 a.m. knowing Brodie and Olsen a little bit, but wondering if we were ever going to complete the process of recruiting Chet Simmons. Even at this point, I wasn't convinced Simmons was the right man for the job. However, he was Evey's choice, and that was that.

Monday, July 23
Plainville, Connecticut

"Bill, wait 'til you see this!" said Dennis Randall, our Public Relations Director, waving a copy of the latest *Sports Illustrated*.

Well, there it was . . . picture and all . . . we were ecstatic! This marked the first major consumer exposure for our fledgling network. We had been receiving considerable attention from trade publications, such as *Advertising Age:*

"The Entertainment and Sports Programming Network, Inc., has just signed a $1,000,000-plus cable TV sponsorship contract with Anheuser-Busch . . . D'Arcy, McManus and Masius, New

York, made the buy for Budweiser and its other beers."

And a sports publication, *The Sporting News:*

"The biggest televised sports story of the week and the year, too, occurred in little Plainville, Connecticut, last Monday. The message was that Big Oil diversified into TV sports."

SI, however, gave America's sports fans a new name ... sports junkies ... from Scott's quote, "What we're creating here is a network for sports junkies. This is not a network for soft-core sports fans who like to watch the NFL and then switch to news ..." *SI* also gave our new network a tremendous boost in prestige and promised America's sports junkies:

"ESPN may become the biggest thing in TV sports since Monday Night Football and night-time World Series games."

Everyone connected with ESPN really got a lift from this first national exposure, and I received phone calls and letters with copies of the article from people all over the country. It was simply great public relations for us as well as the cable industry.

I said everyone was pleased ... well, almost everyone! Evey called as soon as he read the story and said it was the worst piece of reporting he had ever seen. What he really meant was that he wasn't even mentioned. The magic of the story from the writer's perspective was the immense size of our proposed network: "... a nonstop telethon that will ultimately result in 8,760 hours of annual programming—every possible hour, and seven times as many hours as the three major networks combined now air in an average year . . ."

SI's Johnson also spoke of the birth of the concept and summarized our plans, but never mentioned Getty Oil after the first paragraph. Evey's name was nowhere to be found. At first, I thought he was kidding me, but subsequently discovered that national recognition was one major item Evey sought from this TV project. Having missed an opportunity such as *SI* definitely did not please him. It certainly didn't help our personal relationship any. More on that later.

Evey may have been bristling, but ESPN was bustling. Construction in Bristol was on target, but we were forced to expand in Plainville as well. Jim Dovey had unleashed a monster when he rented us our first tiny office in July 1978. We had moved out of that small office into Bob Beyus' original space along with another similar office, and then we rented the hallway. We really did! Jim needed *some* space of his own, so we made a deal to rent the hallway and turn it into one more office and a reception area. Still growing, we agreed to finish some expansion space Jim had on the second floor opposite his conference room. Before we were able to move to Bristol, we had not only moved into the expansion space, but we took over United's conference room and then went into a back room that had been used as warehouse space. By the time we moved into this area, we were too busy to worry about finishing it, so the telephone cords and electrical wiring were dangling from the ceiling and running around poles and under desks—it was a sight to behold.

While the physical problems of finding room for everyone to sit were being solved, ESPN continued to draw more attention from the press. *Connecticut Magazine* scheduled a cover story for the September issue to coincide with our launch. *Business Week* booked an August 1 interview, and *TV Guide* wanted to do a piece. Several newspapers were also lining up coverage for our launch. *Newsweek* said they would do something in the fall, and the cable trades rarely let a week pass without some news of ESPN.

The media fires were further fueled by the now-constant rumors of the imminent hiring of a major network personality. They all felt we were about to unveil a popular national announcer when we dropped our July 31 bombshell of the defection of Chet Simmons from NBC to ESPN.

Tuesday, July 31
Plainville, Connecticut

No press release was made in advance, but Chet Simmons actually arrived in Plainville and went on the ESPN payroll on the last day of

July. Following his weekend visit with Evey in Los Angeles, Chet and his attorney continued a three-cornered discussion with Evey and me. Finally, during a phone call from his home on Tuesday, July 24, Chet agreed to become President of ESPN on July 31. The hangup had been Evey's decision to have me retain the President's title and make Chet Executive Vice President. Chet balked at going from President of NBC Sports to Executive Vice President of an unknown cable network. Egos and reputations in the tiny world of New York television are very fragile.

After meeting with Chet in Los Angeles, Evey tried for another day or two to change Chet's mind, and finally called me to ask, "How does 'William F. Rasmussen, Chairman of the Board' sound? Kind of has a nice ring to it, don't you think?" What choice did I have? We weren't even on the air, and I was already being eased out.

"Sure, fine with me," I answered without enthusiasm.

"Then we can make Chet President and get to work on hiring a staff. Why don't you call Chet and see what he says?" Evey finished.

I called Chet, and he accepted with little delay. We made plans to talk the next day and solve the remaining minor problems. Chet arrived bright and early to take the reins on July

31. It turned out to be a very difficult day for all of us.

The first thing Chet didn't like was his office arrangement. We didn't have much room, as you know, so we put him in a 10' by 12' office with Scott and me. This was Bob Beyus' old office, which adds a touch of irony to our tale. Chet, the NBC heavyweight, was assigned the same desk that Bob had occupied when, one year earlier, he had proclaimed his defection from the E.S.P. Network.

The second thing Chet didn't like was a phone conversation he overheard between Scott and *TV Guide* reporter Rick Cohen. He immediately announced that we not only had to stop talking to reporters indiscriminately, but we could have only one company spokesman. I figured, fine, I'll do it, but I found out later that Chet had other plans.

The third thing Chet didn't like was the fact that Scott, all of 23 years old, was driving a company-financed white Cadillac Coupe de Ville. Like Evey, Chet never gave Scott any credit for his contributions and, in fact, was anxious to have him out of ESPN altogether.

"If he were my son, I'd put him in a Toyota, and he'd pay for it," he grumbled.

The fourth and final negative thing from Chet's point of view was that scheduled telephone interview with *Business Week*. The publication didn't even know Chet would be on board when the interview was scheduled, but that didn't make any difference . . . he wanted to do it instead of me. He didn't . . . I did, but it set the stage for a friction-filled month of August; in reality, Chet and I never developed a strong respect for each other.

He came from the relatively anonymous, yet powerful, post of President of NBC Sports, and here I was, getting national media attention and I was a "nobody" in Chet's jaded view of the TV world. It bothered him, and it bothered Evey. Ultimately, after I was out of the picture, these two personalities clashed over the same issue, and you know who won. Chet's contract was not renewed after three years, and Evey still runs ESPN with an iron hand where public relations are concerned. He has achieved his dream of recognition of sorts, but he's still Getty's Non-Oil Division Vice President.

Wednesday, August 1
Plainville, Connecticut

A company meeting to introduce Chet to all of our employees (now numbering 32) gave no indication of his rocky first day on the job. Matter of fact, he even went out of his way to explain, "I'm here to do a job . . . to run this network and get us on the air September 7. I'll leave all the public image making and press aggrandizement to others (a direct reference to Scott and me) while we do what has to be done. I'm going to ask you

to work hard, to work together and to understand the difficult task we have ahead of us. I'm
delighted to be here and look forward to getting
to know each of you and to working with you on
this project. The ESPN concept of television
sports 24 hours a day is an exciting challenge for
me. I was there during the inception of ABC
Sports and the rebirth of NBC Sports, and I see
many similarities between those beginnings and
the beginning of ESPN. Now, let's get to work.
Thank you all!"

Tuesday, August 7
Bristol, Connecticut
Launch minus 30 days

Chet quickly moved out of his offices in
Plainville and into the Farmington Motor Inn.
Living there while awaiting his house closing in
West Hartford, he decided to use the motel as an
office as well as sleeping quarters. He wasn't
really all that interested in the Bristol construction. He was busy hiring people and trying to
improve our meager program fare for our launch.

He was, therefore, unavailable as Scientific
Atlanta personnel arrived to install our two
10-meter earth stations—our uplinks to Satcom
I. This was a significant day in ESPN's pre-
launch history because, although the building
was progressing nicely, the giant (10 meters in
diameter) earth stations on their remote-con-
trolled mounts, towering in front of our Broad-

cast Center, showed the world we meant business. Until the appearance of this space-age equipment, the local population had little reason to think ESPN was any different from any other small business moving into the redevelopment area on Middle Street.*

Most of the population were delighted. One former mayor running for re-election, however, raised a spectre of disaster. Frank Longo, perennial mayoral candidate, stated, "The radiation from those dishes will kill anything that's nearby. Birds flying too close in front of them will be fried, and there will be a pile of dead birds at the base of each dish." Now, you might think that sounds pretty ridiculous. I know I thought so, but remember, in 1978 domestic satellite communications were just arriving on the scene, and inflammatory statements such as the candidate's were cause for worry for many people. Fortunately for ESPN, we had long before brought Jim Black, a senior Scientific Atlanta engineer, to Bristol to reassure the Redevelopment Authority of the safety of the uplink operations. Longo's comments did provide good copy in the local press, however!

Despite the outrageous comments about radiation, the installation proceeded smoothly, and,

---

* ESPN's actual location is 935 Middle St., Bristol, CT. For national image and publicity purposes, we sought and received permission from the Bristol Postmaster to use "ESPN Plaza" as the official mailing address.

within a week, we actually relayed a signal from the partially completed satellite control room in the partially completed Broadcast Center to Satcom I. Now, all we had to do was finish enough of the building to put a program together to send to the satellite.

Wednesday, August 15
Bristol, Connecticut
Launch minus 22 days

Remember Chet's comments on August 1 about ". . . leaving public image making and press aggrandizement to others . . . ?" Well, he apparently changed his mind because he had Joey Goldstein, a New York PR man, come to Plainville to talk about publicizing both ESPN and Chet in the New York press (although not necessarily in that order). Unbelievably, Evey approved a one-year contract for Joey, and Chet launched his personal PR campaign.

The timing wasn't the best, though, because shortly after the meeting, *Connecticut* magazine hit the newsstands with my picture on the cover and the headline "Why are ABC, CBS and NBC afraid of this man?" Simmons was not happy; Evey was not happy; and I was, unknowingly, a step closer to total alienation from both men. Evey and Simmons still couldn't understand why the media kept talking to Scott and me, and why no one was beating a path to their respective doors. It seemed as if the less we tried, the more publicity we got. The harder Chet tried, the more frustrated he became because he received little notice in the national press and only an acknowledgment in the cable trade papers. All of this changed in the months ahead when Chet finally eliminated Scott from ESPN and directly ordered me not to talk to the press.

Even that didn't stem the publicity tide, and shortly after launch Scott and I, complete with picture, appeared in *Newsweek*. *Cablevision*, an industry publication, did a feature story on ESPN, and I was again on the cover. *TVC*, another cable trade, did a feature story, complete with pictures of all of us (Chet included). The *New York Times* did two articles . . . my picture again . . . and finally *Adweek*, another of the advertising community's trade magazines, named their "Newsmakers of 1979." The sub-headline was "Twelve of the biggest headline makers of the year." You guessed it . . . I was included and Chet wasn't! That was kind of a fun listing since the company included NBC's President Fred Silverman, *The Tonight Show's* Johnny Carson, *Tomorrow's* Tom Snyder, Robin Williams (ABC's Mork), and WTBS-TV's irrepressible Ted Turner.

Thursday, August 23
Bristol, Connecticut
Launch minus 16 days

Chet had hired nearly two dozen former NBC colleagues and dozens of local TV people, as well as a few from other parts of the country. His best pick by far was his former NBC Executive Producer, Alan B. (Scotty) Connal. Scotty was with NBC 32 years and is generally credited with developing the "instant replay" concept we all take for granted today. Scotty is a virtually inexhaustible man and incredibly talented. Without him, ESPN simply would not have been launched on September 7. Scotty was everywhere—hiring people . . . solving problems . . . calming Chet down. In my opinion, he was and is the most important employee ever hired by ESPN.

Sid Petersen, Getty's President, made his first visit to Connecticut on this 23rd day of August. Sid is an extremely competent and talented oil industry executive. Today, he is Getty's Chairman. At an informal cocktail party for employees the evening of his visit, he said, "I wish I could bottle up this enthusiasm and take it back to Getty."

He was absolutely right! While Chet, Scott, Stu and I had our internal skirmishes, the level of dedication and enthusiasm among all the other employees was unbelievable. Every time someone said we'd never be on the air by

September 7, the entire group seemed to work harder, as if to say, "Want to bet?"

George Conner has this observation of those frantic days:

"New people arrived each day and either learned very fast or would just not be around. ESPN had no place for anyone who did not want to work hard. There was too much going on as the company was evolving. I doubt if I will ever witness anything quite like it in my lifetime. Any time I spoke with someone who had not been to the ESPN headquarters in Connecticut, I just told them, 'You have to see it to believe it. There is no way to explain what is going on here.' You could walk through the building without talking to anyone and still feel the excitement everywhere. They were the most dedicated people I've ever worked with. Everyone was dedicated to one purpose: to make ESPN the best sports television network anywhere."

I might add, George was right at the top of the list of those dedicated people and never faltered in his belief in the future success of ESPN.

The week preceding launch was packed with excitement. As soon as Petersen left Connecticut, Evey, Simmons and I headed for Dublin, Ohio, and the Jack Nicklaus designed Muirfield Village Golf Links. Evey had scheduled a meeting of all the non-oil executives under his supervision to meet Chet and explain the ESPN concept, and to give each of the other groups an opportunity to tell both Chet and me what was happening in their areas.

The highlight of the trip for me was the opportunity to play two rounds on the beautiful golf course. Those rounds turned out to be the last ones I played in 1979.

Back to Connecticut for two days of meetings. They included those with Sam Kasparian, the Redevelopment Authority Director, to discuss an additional land purchase and John Toner for an NCAA and UConn update.

Wednesday, Chet and I flew to Los Angeles for a Thursday 8:00 am meeting with the Los Angeles Olympic Organizing Committee (LAOOC) Chairman, Peter Ueberroth, and other committee members. The topic of discussion was ESPN's brash bid for the 1984 Olympic TV rights. We had made our $750,000 deposit for the right to bid, and were in very fast company with only ABC, NBC, CBS and Tandem Productions (Jerry Perenchio and Norman Lear) joining us. Since we were not even on the air, we didn't really receive serious consideration, although Evey made clear to the committee members that money would not be a problem.

Time was winding down in Bristol. Only one week to launch as Chet and I flew back to Connecticut at week's end.

Monday, September 3, Labor Day
Bristol, Connecticut
Launch minus 4 days

"Absolutely no way we'll be on the air Friday," Chet declared. "They haven't even finished the studio. The outside walls on the building aren't complete. How can we do it?"

Now that was a good question! The masons were finishing outside while the insulation and drywall people kept pace inside almost before the mortar was dry. At one point, the painters were actually painting at one end of the building, the insulation and drywall people were in the next room and the masons had yet to finish the outside wall at the far end of the building. It was going to be some week.

Equipment arrived daily, and soon, all the Plainville space was taken. Two video tape machines arrived. There simply was no more air-conditioned space, so Scott suggested they move them into his condo living room and do tape work from there for a few days until they could be moved into the Broadcast Center.

Chet called Scott to task for this . . . ranted and raved at him, actually . . . but Scott's living room was a lot safer and drier than the parking lot.

We met our set designer on Labor Day as well. She showed us a model of what she proposed and, for the only time since I had known him, saw George Conner outmaneuvered on a financial question. He was looking over the model and listening to the explanation and then asked, "How much is all of this going to cost?"

"Plenty!" was the one-word answer that stopped him in his tracks.

Labor Day week was a blur of activity for all of us. People and equipment arrived hourly, and phone calls confirming guests or demanding delivery were seemingly made around the clock. As Thursday turned to evening and we were less than 24 hours from launch, a light note crept into the pressure cooker that was ESPN.

Cecil Coleman, NCAA TV Committee Chairman, and Jim Shaffer, the NCAA/ESPN representative, arrived early and quickly decided to stay out of everyone's way. Good thinking, I might add—they might have been permanently built-in to some part of the Broadcast Center.

Since they represented our major program supplier and were our real road to national recognition, we didn't want them to feel ignored, so Scott, Dennis Randall and Jon Foley decided to take them to dinner and entertain them for the evening.

Scott tells the story:

"There isn't much to do in Plainville, Connecticut, or its bigger neighbor, Bristol. We had dinner in a small restaurant and finished by 9:00 p.m. It was late for dinner in Connecticut, but still too early for us to leave our guests. Dennis suggested a drink at one of the local 'entertainment emporiums.' Now, Plainville, Connecticut, doesn't have a Studio 54 or any flashy big-city clubs, so we ended up at the Rosebud, noted for absolutely nothing, and closed the place at 1:00 am. While the ESPN employees worked through the night, Jon, Dennis and I quietly entertained the Chairman of the powerful NCAA Television Committee at perhaps the worst dive ever to be entered by a man of his stature."

As the clock struck midnight, I left the Broadcast Center and headed for some sleep. With only 19 hours to air time, the studio was still empty, since the set was due to be delivered on the 7th. Engineers were still hanging lights. A hole was being broken in the back wall of the studio to run camera cables from the rented remote van parked out back. Unbelievably, we were going to launch a multi-million dollar network with rented equipment and a part time crew in an incomplete building. September 7 promised to be quite a day! A day not soon forgotten!

Chapter 9

Sports Junkies Rejoice!

Friday, September 7, 1979
Bristol, Connecticut
6:00 a.m.—Launch minus 13 hours

Who can sleep? This is the day we've been waiting for. In 13 hours the dream comes true . . . we hope!! Will it work? Will transponder 7 be ready, as RCA has guaranteed? How can we possibly finish all the little undone things in time? This will be a long and busy day! Evey, Simmons and I will do some tape segments for tonight's opening show. Producer Bill Creasy will try to do a couple of rehearsals with a crew that's never worked together before today. The script isn't even ready. The set has to be finished. Remote satellite feeds from Boulder, Colorado, and Milwaukee, Wisconsin, need to be coordinated. The NCAA representatives and the D'Arcy (Budweiser) people must be entertained. Above all, the incredible confusion that accompanies any partially completed construction project must be cleaned up so that we can get on with the business of television. Yes, it really promises to be a busy day . . .

8:00 a.m.
Launch minus 11 hours

One look at the total chaos prompts Chet to say, "I knew we should have postponed this to January 1. I told you we couldn't be ready."

"We're committed, Chet," I remind him.

"I don't know why I listened to you. I shouldn't have let you talk me into this," he continues.

"We've been over all of that, and there's nothing we can do—we're on the air in less than 11 hours. Let's go to work." I end the conversation.

Remember my optimism from the early days? Well, looking around now, I have to admit that Chet has a point. Things look pretty confused, and, for a fleeting instant, I silently wonder if we will be 'live' at 7 p.m. When I say "fleeting instant", that's exactly what I mean. No looking back . . . forget the pessimism . . . let's go to work!

10:00 a.m.
Launch minus 9 hours

The main corridor of the Broadcast Center is a shambles.

"Anybody seen the Sony guy?" someone shouts.

Sony is to hand-deliver one of their new BVH 1100 Series one-inch tape machines, and we have to have it today. We already received a partial shipment of their old models (which are now mounted on top of the crates in which they arrived), but we need the 1100. As Getty promised, ESPN is a first-class operation, and that means having the latest state-of-the-art equipment.

"What's the taping schedule? Where's Creasy?" another voice asks. "We've got to do a lot of editing. The sooner we shoot the brass, the better." This is a reference to the tapes Evey, Simmons and I are scheduled to do.

"Can't do 'em 'til after lunch!" is the unwelcome answer. The delay adds more time pressures for all concerned.

Noon
Launch minus 7 hours

"Where's Dale Eckert?" Chet screams. "How can I get anything done with all these guys working in here? Doesn't anybody understand that we have a network to launch today?" By now, all who work with Chet are familiar with his outbursts and tirades . . . particularly when the pressure is on.

"We'll be fine, Chet," Scotty reassures him. "The studio will be ready by four, and we'll have a couple of hours for rehearsal."

"I want this place cleaned up!!" Chet again.

Other tempers are beginning to fray a little, and Chet isn't helping things. Chuck Stover, Dale Eckert's construction site chief, tries to calm Chet. "We'll have it cleaned up for you right after lunch."

I've been on the phone with people from all over the country wishing us well. Telegrams are arriving. The local florist has already made two trips to ESPN Plaza with congratulatory arrangements. He'll make several more before the day is over.

1:00 p.m.
Launch minus 6 hours

Still no sign of Dale Eckert or the Sony rep. The script still isn't finished. We still haven't taped a thing. Somebody has the presence of mind to call a local coffee and sandwich service. The driver has to call for reinforcements before an hour has passed. We have over 100 construction people racing the clock and nearly as many television people running a similar race over the same track, so the sandwich business is brisk.

"Bill, Chet, take a look at this script," a harried Bill Creasy asks. "While you're looking at it, Bill, come outside so we can start setting up your interview with Evey."

I glance quickly at the script and discover that, on "someone's" orders, Scott has been written out of this version. Not only written out, he isn't even mentioned. I complain, and he is at least mentioned as one of the co-founders. Both Simmons and Evey still have a problem with the young, 23-year-old co-founder getting the press coverage he is, and they aren't about to add to his credits if they can help it.

"Bill, we'll shoot you and Mr. Evey at 1:30, O.K?"

"Sure!"

We do our little tape piece (in only four takes). Evey says all the obligatory nice things about Getty's association with ESPN, Chet and me. He predicts big things for ESPN and the cable industry and reaffirms Getty's commitment to quality.

2:00 p.m.
Launch minus 5 hours

The Marines have landed! Big Dale Eckert, looking and acting like a tough Marine master sergeant, has arrived and taken over.

"Where have you been? We can't work in this mess," Chet challenges.

"I'll have the building ready for you ... just take care of your television business," is Dale's heated retort. Obviously, he means what he says, and the message gets through to everyone. With a renewed energy—almost frenzy—construction hands and feet begin to fly around the Broadcast Center. Chet backs off.

3:00 p.m.
Launch minus 4 hours

I can't believe where I am! I'm not wild about heights, but Creasy's script has me in a mechanical lift about 25-30 feet off the ground next to one of our 10 meter uplinks for a short explanatory tape piece about how our signal will go from uplink to satellite to downlinks all over America (see illustration, page 49) and into individual cable homes. We do the tape in a hurry, believe me.

4:00 p.m.
Launch minus 3 hours

The set still isn't finished. The Sony man has arrived though. Amidst the turmoil, the remote truck outside the studio is the scene of hectic activity. The camera cables have been run through a hole in the back wall and technicians are checking out the cameras. Working with the available lights will be a bit tricky when we go on the air, since our full lighting grid hasn't been completed.

Creasy has had a production group from New York City on hand to help with various effects he wants to include in the show, and they've put together a mini set for me to explain the "flashlight" theory of satellite coverage in laymen's terms (see illustration, page 51). This piece has to be pre-taped, and time is running out. We have to do it in the studio, and, at the moment, the studio is crammed with other people doing things that they absolutely must do in the studio.

Creasy solves that problem easily. "O.K., everybody, we have to tape a short piece, and we're going to turn out the lights for just a couple of minutes." This is necessary to clearly illustrate the "flashlight footprint." With all the people anxious to get back to the business at hand, you can bet we do that tape in one take.

5:00 p.m.
Launch minus 2 hours

Activity up and down the main corridor of the Broadcast Center and in every room off the corridor is beginning to look like the proverbial "Chinese fire drill." People aren't walking fast any more—they're jogging and running. Eckert, Connell, Creasy and Simmons have all the troops hopping.

Into the midst of this tornado of activity stroll Cecil Coleman and Jim Shaffer of the NCAA. They are in town *officially* to watch our inaugural NCAA football efforts this weekend, and we had invited them to visit with us and be on hand for the opening at 7 p.m. They aren't prepared for the sight that greets them and, though they make no comment, I'm sure they are having some thoughts about the folly of our undertaking at the moment. The folks from D'Arcy haven't arrived yet, but they will certainly have the same kinds of thoughts.

Creasy announces, "We can't do a studio rehearsal until 6:30!" The tension is mounting! No outbursts from anyone though. The adrenalin is flowing, and everyone is watching the clock.

"Chet, we'll do your tape at 5:30," the Crease advises.

"Fine! How's the set coming, Scotty?" Chet inquires.

"We'll be ready. The paint may still be wet and the drapes in motion, but we'll be ready." Scotty's confidence and competence reassure the troops.

Creasy again, "Anybody seen Bill Flynn?" (he's the President of the NCAA and will do a live interview during the opening show).

"He's out front with the other NCAA guys." This from a passing technician.

"Somebody ask him to come in here so we can set up his interview. I don't think we'll have time to talk to him once we get into the studio."

6:00 p.m.
Launch minus one hour

One more sweep of the hour hand and we're "live." Will it work? Will we be ready? Sure! At this moment, there's no turning back . . . it better work!! The frantic peak reached a couple of hours ago continues, but with more and more confidence. That "enthusiasm" Sid Peterson mentioned a month ago is really shining through. Proud, talented and creative people are answering a challenge! A challenge beset with enormous logistical problems, but a challenge to be conquered in less than an hour.

Not much for Scott and me to do now but wait, and we find ourselves taking one last walk around the site. Less than six months ago, ground was broken. The skeptics said we'd never make it by September 7, and yet, here we are. The efforts of literally thousands of people will culminate in our first regular transmission in about 50 minutes.

As Scott and I circle the building, we don't say much—each lost in his own thoughts. Thoughts of the future! Thoughts of the recent past! Thoughts of each other. I can't tell you how many times I asked this 23 year old man to take on responsibilities that would have made a mature veteran falter. Ah, the exuberance and confidence of youth. We find ourselves at the deserted north side of the building, and we just stop and look at each other. It's a moment I'll never forget! Without a word, we suddenly put our arms around each other and tears begin to flow—tears of happiness; tears of pride; tears of love. We do finally exchange a few comments, which I prefer to keep to myself. Before walking back into the Broadcast Center, we speak briefly of the awesome capability we are about to begin utilizing on a regular basis at 7 p.m. The capability to instantly deliver sports television to every corner of America. From 7 p.m. forward, cable television, sports television and the way people watch sports television will never be the same. Life for Scott and me will never be the same either.

6:30 p.m.
Launch minus 30 minutes

"O.K., Lee, we'll fade the theme under and then cue you for your opening comments," says the director. "We can't play the theme cart (music cartridge) right now, but just go ahead, and we'll do what we can."

The D'Arcy people have arrived . . . a full contingent of D'Arcy people—Gene Petrillo, Dick Simon, et al. Our future production control room overlooking the studio is packed with some pretty high-powered spectators eagerly awaiting the 7:00 p.m. launch. Lots of hand-shaking and nervous laughter! Everyone present has some heavy stakes riding on a successful launch. A lot of reputations will be on the line when we go live.

"Camera 2, you're too tight," the director's voice piped into the control room for our guests reminds us that the rehearsal is under way in the studio.

6:40 p.m.
Launch minus 20 minutes

Colin Fox, our satellite technical supervisor, reports, "Vernon Valley confirms saturation for transponder 7." Colin has conducted extensive tests with the RCA Vernon Valley Satellite Center for the past several days. The Scientific Atlanta people have been babysitting their newly installed uplinks and, as they say, "all systems are go." Up to now, we've only been testing. Even though we know everything will be fine, a growing excitement throughout the Broadcast Center is fueled by the unknown . . . by the knowledge that in minutes we'll stop testing and become a new network. It has to work!

6:45 p.m.
Launch minus 15 minutes

"Lee, we won't have time for any Flynn rehearsal." The director's voice is coming through the control room speakers to remind everyone that we're running out of time. "Show him where he'll sit and remind him he comes in and sits down during the first break."

Creasy, "Are we set with the Fairbanks feed from Boulder?"

Fox, "We're monitoring them now. Looks and sounds good."

"How about the ball game?" This is in reference to the softball World Series in which the

Milwaukee Schlitz will compete on our first live remote broadcast . . . a broadcast sponsored by Budweiser. A few of us squirmed a bit when Milwaukee won the right to play, as you might well imagine.

6:48 p.m.
Launch minus 12 minutes

The director's detached voice again, "Twelve minutes to air. Lee, we have to clear the studio. Everything looks good. Take a few minutes, check your make-up, and be back at :55."

People are literally running to deliver tape, set a light, reposition a chair, straighten a drape . . . a thousand little details are getting immediate attention. During this temporary respite, and because the crowd in the control room makes pacing the floor a difficult task, several people move into the central corridor and into a swirl of activity.

6:50 p.m.
Launch minus 10 minutes

Unbelievably, the clean-up job is continuing with launch only 10 minutes away. Dale Eckert has reduced the size of his work force to lessen the chaos, but you'd never know it by the numbers of bodies moving up and down the corridor.

In the midst of all this, I notice a window-washer with his spray and squeegee, cleaning all the glass doors that line the west side of the corridor. I nod to Dale, who shrugs his shoulders, and then someone asks the window-washer, "Hey, what are you doing? We're going on the air in a few minutes."

Totally unflustered and obviously unimpressed by all this TV hubbub, the window-washer answers, "I was told to do the doors, and I just got around to it. I'm only doing what I'm told." He obviously has his priorities straight.

6:55 p.m.
Launch minus 5 minutes

"We've got live feeds from Colorado and the ball park," Fox reports.

Everyone is back in the control room. Evey, Simmons, Scott and I, Petrillo, Simon, Coleman, Shaffer and seemingly a hundred more. Stomach muscles are tightening just a bit. Throats are becoming just a little scratchy. Tempers are taut, and everyone in the room is helpless to alter the course of whatever events are about to happen.

6:57 p.m.
Launch minus 3 minutes

Voices are tumbling out of the control room speaker. Before any TV show, the apparently disorganized confusion is enough to make any uninitiated spectator wonder how anything good will ever be done. In reality, everyone in the studio, the tape room, the remote truck and the engineering center is doing his individual job with a time deadline very well in mind. Just before air time, the director will get everyone off the in-house communication system and take command.

"Three minutes to air." This is a new voice that Creasy has assigned to keep everyone informed of the exact time remaining to launch so that he, his director and crew can be free to talk to each other.

"Is everybody in the studio?" the director asks.

"All here," a cameraman answers.

"Tape room?"

"Ready!"

"Satellite?"

"Ready!"

Conversation is concise and crisp. The emotion almost squeaks through the speaker over our heads.

6:58 p.m.
Launch minus 2 minutes

"Two minutes to launch," says the timekeeper.

Creasy orders, "Everybody not involved in the opening show, please leave the studio."

"Ninety seconds to launch," the timekeeper.

Nervous fingers check, check and recheck settings on camera control units, VTR's, audio levels, uplink levels, and on and on.

6:59 p.m.
Launch minus 1 minute

The director takes over, "One minute to air. Looking good, Lee. Stand by! VTR?"

"VTR O.K.!

"Audio?"

"Audio, check."

"Satellite?"

"Video and audio confirmed by Vernon Valley."

"Thirty seconds to air. Stand by in the studio."

"Stand by audio theme cart."

"Camera one, a little tighter, please. We open with you."

"Lee, you'll take your cue from the A.D. next to Camera one. We can't get the IFB (communications) to your headset." Lee nods.

"Twenty seconds."

Sweaty palms for several of us in the control room. I can't decide whether the second hand is moving too fast or too slow. The tension is immense. No more nervous conversation. No conversation at all! We're all transfixed by the scene on the other side of the glass. We're all watching Lee Leonard, and waiting.

"Ten seconds."

"Stand by to roll theme."

"Stand by Camera one. Good luck, everybody."

"Five seconds to air, Lee."

"Three."

"Two."

"One."

7:00 p.m.
Launch

"Take one and roll theme."

"Theme under and . . . cue Lee."

"If you love sports . . . if you **REALLY** love sports, you'll think you've died and gone to sports heaven . . . "

Epilog

7:00:20 p.m.
Launch plus 20 seconds

A touch at my elbow brought my thoughts back to the control room, and, as I turned to see who was seeking my attention, I discovered Scott with two glasses of champagne. "We did it! Congratulations, Dad!"

"And the same to you," I answered.

The control room was packed with other people, but Scott had saved his final personal touch for the exact moment of launch and popped the cork on the champagne bottle at precisely 7:00 p.m. As we toasted each other, neither of us could guess what lay ahead, but we certainly knew what had gone into making this launch possible. No matter what the future held, we were extremely proud and very lucky to have accomplished so much from such a modest beginning.

7:01 p.m.
Launch plus one minute

"RCA says video and audio perfect, congratulations, ESPN!" reported Colin Fox.

This report brought smiles all around, but the tension remained. A lot of things have to go right, and one good minute does not a network make. We would be on the air for the next 58 consecutive hours . . . plenty of time for things to go wrong. Far too early to offer too many congratulatory comments.

7:02 p.m.
Launch plus two minutes

"Where's the audio?" the disembodied voice of the director asked.

"Western Union's lost it!" Colin Fox answered. "We had it until just before air."

This exchange was occasioned by the Chuck Fairbanks interview from Boulder, Colorado. The video was fine, but there was no sound.

"Cue Lee. During the break I'll fill him in, and, if we get the sound, we'll try it later in the show."

Western Union did correct the problem, and we did get that Fairbanks interview later in the half-hour. Everything else went pretty well. The taped pieces we had done earlier in the day worked; Lee Leonard's interview with Bill Flynn was fine and the NCAA Preview Show went well. Before we knew it, we were into our first live

event: the Professional Softball World Series
with the Milwaukee Schlitz.

8:00 p.m.
Launch plus 60 minutes

ESPN's first live event brought more chuckles
from the D'Arcy people and some nervous
laughter from us for the obvious reasons:
Budweiser sponsored the show. We survived,
though, and went on into the evening schedule
and straight through to Monday morning, com-
pleting our first 58 hours of non-stop sports
without too many serious hitches.*

8:10 p.m.
Launch plus 70 minutes

A launch party was now in full swing at the
Plainville Holiday Inn. United Cable of
Plainville had wired several monitors to the
party room so that everyone not directly connected with the launch could watch and get an
early start on the festivities.

People began to drift away from the Broadcast
Center about 8:00 p.m. to go to the Holiday Inn
and spend the evening relaxing from the tensions
and anxieties of the day. We were on the air! We

---

* For comparison, the Appendix includes ESPN's first
week's actual schedule as well as the actual schedule for
the same time period in September, 1982. You will note
the upgraded quality of the programming in three short
years.

met our self-imposed deadline! However, relaxing for some of us was tough.

Brief party appearances by Chet, Scotty, Scott and me ended with a trip back to the Bristol Broadcast Center "just to watch—feel—observe—and even enjoy a bit of delayed excitement." Everything was proceeding on schedule—makeshift control room and all! Critics had quite a bit to say about the programming, the people, and the facilities, but critics or not, ESPN was alive and taking the first tentative steps toward becoming the largest cable programming service in America.

The days immediately following launch were especially difficult for the original E.S.P. Network employees, myself included. On the Sunday following launch, Simmons, Evey and I had breakfast. During that brief meeting Evey, in no uncertain terms, told me, "Chet's in charge. You stay out of his way!"

A week later, Simmons informed Scott that Evey wanted to talk to him. Scott called Getty's headquarters and was invited to come to Los Angeles "to discuss his future with ESPN." Some future! Some offer! Evey's "offer" to Scott was a 75 percent cut in pay to stay with the company and learn the business from the bottom up. Scott was gone by October 1st.

The same pattern applied to other "originals." Bob Bray was "offered" a new post at 50% of his former salary. Jon Foley was terminated in

November by "mutual agreement," and Bob Chamberlain was not even given the courtesy of an "offer." He was just terminated.

Peter Fox and I lasted about a year. The standard "offer" didn't work very well with us, but, eventually, we succumbed and "resigned." The same is true of Bob Ronstrom. My brother, Don, stayed on through January 1980 before he submitted his resignation.

Lou Palmer was the only survivor, and, at this writing, is still doing a strong, professional job for the network.

While the "exodus of originals" was under way, an "NBC immigration" was taking place. During Simmons' first 60 days nearly two dozen former NBC compatriots were recruited to fill a variety of posts. Most appointees were very competent, and many remain at ESPN today.

Through all of the personnel machinations, ESPN has continued to grow. On April 14, 1980, the programming was expanded to include many more weekday daytime hours. On September 1, 1980, the network moved to fulfill its original promise to the cable industry and began providing sports programming 24 hours a day, 7 days a week, 8,760 hours a year.

On the affiliate side, growth has been spectacular. Delivered via satellite, ESPN reached into 6 million homes in December 1980; 12 million in December 1981; nearly 20 million in December 1982; and projections indicate ESPN will be seen in just under 30 million homes by December 1983, thereby surpassing Ted Turner's Atlanta Superstation as the most widely distributed cable signal in America.

Advertisers have flocked to the network as well. To D'Arcy's initial Anheuser-Busch buy in January 1979, over 300 major U.S. corporations have added their advertising commitments.

Today, in addition to the NCAA, ESPN boasts contracts with the NBA and the USFL. Weekly boxing was reunited with TV through a Bob Arum Pact in early 1980.

Perhaps the biggest programming success story to be told is the NCAA basketball playoff package on ESPN. Each year, beginning in 1980, ESPN has done at least 22 NCAA playoff basketball telecasts. This has expanded NCAA playoff coverage tremendously, and ESPN has given national exposure to scores of the finest student athletes in America who were formerly seen only on their hometown local TV station.

The same is true of the playoffs for NCAA Divisions Two and Three basketball, Divisions One and Two hockey and the college baseball World Series. The marriage of sports and ESPN has generally worked very well for all concerned.

What began as the dream of a couple of "little guys from Connecticut" has grown into a major business for the town of Bristol, Connecticut, a major subsidiary for the Getty Oil Company, a major program service for the cable industry, and a major advertising vehicle for national advertisers. Most of all, our "dream" has become reality for the sports fans of America . . . that incredible army of which you are a part!

So, while the tumult and the shouting fade into history, and "the thrill of victory and the agony of defeat" make only weekend appearances, **ESPN** shines daily as the place "where the cheering never stops."

Here's to you, sports junkies . . . **REJOICE!!!**

Glossary

ABC — American Broadcasting Company. One of the three major television broadcast networks in America with CBS and NBC.

ATC — American Television and Communications. An American major cable multiple-system-operator.

AT&T — American Telephone and Telegraph.

Anik — Communications satellite serving Canada.

Basic Cable — A packaged service of selected television signals, both local and microwave or satellite-delivered, available to subscribers at a basic monthly subscription fee.

Bicycling	A prearranged pattern of shipping programs and commercials from station to station or cable system to cable system by ordinary mail or freight.
Bird	Industry term for any satellite. "RCA bird," "Westar bird."
Cable	A television, audio and/or data delivery system that uses wire for signal transmissions to individual homes within a franchise area instead of over the air.
CATV	Community Antenna Television, i.e., cable TV.
CBS	Columbia Broadcasting System, Inc. One of the three major broadcast television networks in America with ABC and NBC.
Channel Capacity	The number of channels (television signals) a cable television system can deliver to its subscribers.
Dedicated Channel	A cable channel delivering programming from a single source.
Dish	Industry slang for earth receiving station.

Downlink   Technically, the return of a
                    satellite signal from the satel-
                    lite to earth. Also commonly
                    used for earth receiving sta-
                    tion.

Earth Station   A parabolic antenna (dish) re-
                    quired to receive and/or send
                    electronic signals (video,
                    audio, data etc.) from or to a
                    communications satellite.

ESPN   The Entertainment and Sports
                    Programming Network, Inc.
                    The Total Sports Network.
                    The largest pure cable
                    network in America capable of
                    being received in nearly 30
                    million homes. (Source: A.C.
                    Nielsen Company.)

Footprint   The area on earth in which a
                    viewable satellite signal can
                    be received.

Franchise   The contract between a specific
                    government body and a cable
                    television service granting the
                    exclusive right to install cable
                    within a specific geographic
                    area.

Geosynchronous   An orbital path 22,300 miles
Orbit   above the equator, where a
                    satellite can travel at the
                    same relative speed as the
                    earth, thus making it appear

to be stationary in relation to a fixed spot on earth.

HBO   Home Box Office. The largest of all cable pay networks. A service of Time, Inc.

Interconnect   Two or more cable systems in the same geographic area joined together to pool programs of local interest and/or sell advertising of regional interest.

MSG   Madison Square Garden. Famed New York sports arena Also sports programming network delivering events from Madison Square Garden to the New York market and surrounding area as well as providing many events to the USA network for national distribution.

MSO   Multiple System Operator. A company owning two or more cable systems. Largest five in America are: ATC, Group W, TCI, Cox, and Warner/Amex.

NBC   National Broadcasting Company. One of the three major television broadcast networks with ABC and CBS.

NCTA   National Cable Television Association. The National trade

association of the cable industry.

Pay Cable — Specialized programming for which an individual sub-scriber pays an additional monthly charge above the basic fee to his local cable sys-tem.

Prime Time — Peak television viewing hours.

RCA Americom — Domestic satellite communica-tions division of RCA Corporation. Launches and maintains Satcom series of domestic satellites. Satcom 3R is the primary cable televi-sion bird while Satcom IV is designated Cable Net II.

Satcom — Name given to all domestic com-munications satellites launched, owned and operated by RCA Americom.

Scientific Atlanta, Inc. — Major manufacturer of earth station antennas (dishes) and other satellite communica-tions related equipment.

Subscriber — Individual home (business) pay-ing a monthly fee for cable television service.

TCI — Telecommunications, Inc. One of the largest multiple-system-operators in the country.

TVRO — A receive-only earth station.

Transponder   The portion of a communica-
               tions satellite that receives
               and retransmits specific video
               and audio signals. All satel-
               lites serving the cable indus-
               try today carry 24 transpon-
               ders—channels, if you will.

Uplink   The television, audio or data
               signal on its way from an
               earth transmitter to a satel-
               lite. Also, commonly used to
               designate an earth transmit-
               ting station.

USA Network   The 24-hour cable television
               network spawned by Madison
               Square Garden Sports. Today,
               in addition to sports, the
               network carries programs of
               interest to women, along with
               documentaries and other en-
               tertainment shows.

Westar   Name given to all domestic com-
               munications   satellites
               launched, owned and operated
               by Western Union.

Appendix

COMPARATIVE SCHEDULES
ESPN'S First Week of Programming
September 7-14, 1979

07:00 PM	PREMIERE SHOW LIVE, FROM ESPN STUDIO IN BRISTOL, CONNECTICUT
07:30 PM	NCAA PREVIEW
08:00 PM	SLOW-PITCH WORLD SERIES #1 & SLO-PITCH WORLD SERIES #2 (one game featured Kentucky Bourbons vs. Milwaukee Schlitzes, sponsored by Anheuser-Busch)
11:00 PM	FILA WRESTLING #1
11:30 PM	SPORTS RECAP (named SPORTSCENTER on September 11, 1979)
12:00 AM	NCAA SOCCER: UCLA @ ST. LOUIS
02:00 AM	PREMIERE SHOW (2nd Air)
02:30 AM	NCAA PREVIEW (2nd Air)
03:00 AM	MONTE CARLO TENNIS

September 8, 1979

07:00 AM	MUNSTER HURLING
08:00 AM	FILA WRESTLING #1 (2nd Air)
08:30 AM	IRISH CYCLING
09:00 AM	SPORTS RECAP

09:30 AM	SLO-PITCH WORLD SERIES #1 (2nd Air)
	SLO-PITCH WORLD SERIES #2 (2nd Air)
12:30 PM	MEN'S VOLLEYBALL: KOREA VS. JAPAN
03:00 PM	MARATHON: A PERSONAL TEST
03:30 PM	NCAA SOCCER: UCLA VS. U CONN
05:30 PM	FILA WRESTLING #2
06:00 PM	SPORTS RECAP
06:30 PM	WOMEN'S VOLLEYBALL: USA VS. USSR
08:00 PM	SLO-PITCH WORLD SERIES #3
	SLO-PITCH WORLD SERIES #4
11:00 PM	SPORTS RECAP
11:30 PM	LPGA GOLF: SAHARA OPEN

September 9, 1979

01:30 AM	NCAA FOOTBALL: OREGON @ COLORADO
04:30 AM	SLO-PITCH ALL-STAR GAME #1
06:00 AM	NCAA SOCCER: UCLA @ ST. LOUIS (2nd Air)
08:00 AM	SLO-PITCH ALL-STAR GAME #2
09:30 AM	SPORTS RECAP
10:00 AM	NCAA FOOTBALL:
	S. CAROLINA @ N. CAROLINA
01:00 PM	MOSS CREEK GOLF—ROUNDS 1 & 2
04:00 PM	SLO-PITCH WORLD SERIES #3 (2nd Air)
05:30 PM	WOMEN'S VOLLEYBALL:
	USA VS. USSR (2nd Air)
07:00 PM	SPORTS RECAP
07:30 PM	NCAA FOOTBALL:
	OREGON @ COLORADO (2nd Air)
10:00 PM	SPORTS RECAP
11:00 PM	NCAA FOOTBALL:
	VILLANOVA @ MARYLAND

September 10, 1979

02:00 AM	NCAA FOOTBALL: GRAMBLING VS.
	MORGAN ST.
05:00 AM	SPORTS RECAP
06:00 PM	SPORTS RECAP
06:30 PM	SPORTS HOTLINE
07:00 PM	NCAA FOOTBALL HIGHLIGHTS

07:30 PM   NCAA FOOTBALL: GRAMBLING VS.
           MORGAN ST. (2nd Air)
10:30 PM   FILA WRESTLING #3
11:00 PM   SPORTS HOTLINE
11:30 PM   NCAA FOOTBALL HIGHLIGHTS

September 11, 1979

12:00 AM   SLO-PITCH WORLD SERIES #4 (2nd Air)
01:30 AM   SOCCER: UCLA @ U CONN (2nd Air)
03:30 AM   SPORTS RECAP
06:00 PM   SPORTS RECAP
06:30 PM   SPORTS HOTLINE
07:00 PM   NCAA FOOTBALL:
           VILLANOVA @ MARYLAND (2nd Air)
09:45 PM   HURLING
11:00 PM   SPORTSCENTER
11:30 PM   SPORTS HOTLINE

September 12, 1979

12:00 AM   FILA WRESTLING #3 (2nd Air)
12:30 AM   SOCCER: ST. LOUIS @ U CONN
03:00 AM   SPORTSCENTER
06:00 PM   SPORTSCENTER
06:30 PM   SPORTS HOTLINE
07:00 PM   NCAA FOOTBALL:
           S. CAROLINA @ N. CAROLINA (2nd Air)
10:00 PM   NCAA SOCCER:
           SUI EDWARDSVILLE @ SEATTLE PACIFIC

September 13, 1979

12:00 AM   SPORTSCENTER
12:30 AM   SPORTS HOTLINE
01:00 AM   NCAA SOCCER:
           SANTA CLARA @ WASHINGTON
03:00 AM   SPORTSCENTER
06:00 PM   SPORTSCENTER
06:30 PM   SPORTS HOTLINE
07:00 PM   MEN'S VOLLEYBALL:
           KOREA VS. JAPAN (2nd Air)
09:30 PM   DAVIS CUP HIGHLIGHTS

11:00 PM   SPORTS CENTER
11:30 PM   NCAA SOCCER:
           SANTA CLARA @ WASHINGTON (2nd Air)

September 14, 1979

02:00 AM   NCAA SOCCER:
           ST. LOUIS @ U CONN (2nd Air)
03:30 AM   SPORTSCENTER
04:45 PM   SPORTSCENTER
05:00 PM   DAVIS CUP TENNIS—SINGLES
10:00 PM   AMERICAN SLO-PITCH #5
11:30 PM   AMERICAN SLO-PITCH #6

ESPN PROGRAMMING
SEPTEMBER 7-14, 1982

September 7, 1982

12:00 AM   ESPN Presents Saturday Night at the Fights:
           Main Event—Roberto Duran vs. Kirkland Laing
02:30 AM   SportsCenter
03:30 AM   ESPN's Inside Baseball
04:00 AM   CFL Football: Edmonton @ Calgary
06:30 AM   "Down The Stretch" ESPN's Horse Racing
           Weekly
07:00 AM   SportsCenter
09:00 AM   ESPN's Inside Baseball
09:30 AM   International Racquetball Championships:
           Women's First Round—Match #1—
           Suzie Dugan vs. Linda Forcade
10:00 AM   SportsCenter
12:00 AM   College Football: Temple @ Penn State
03:00 PM   ESPN's Inside Baseball
03:30 PM   "Down The Stretch": ESPN's Horse Racing
           Weekly
04:00 PM   CFL Football: Montreal @ Hamilton
06:30 PM   NCAA Instructional Series:
           Volleyball—Passing, Setting, and Spiking
06:45 PM   NASL Weekly
07:15 PM   NCAA Instructional Series: Soccer-Shooting
07:30 PM   SportsCenter

08:00 PM   Exhibition Basketball: NBA All-Stars vs. Chinese
           Army Team from Shanghai, China
10:00 PM   Unlimited Hydroplane Racing: The Columbia
           Cup From Tri Cities, WA
11:00 PM   SportsCenter

September 8, 1982

12:00 AM   College Football: Temple @ Penn State
03:00 AM   SportsCenter
04:00 AM   CFL Football: Montreal @ Hamilton
06:30 AM   NASL Weekly
07:00 AM   SportsCenter
09:00 AM   Unlimited Hydroplane Racing: The Columbia Cup
10:00 AM   SportsCenter
12:00 PM   ESPN's SportsWoman
12:30 PM   International Racquetball Championships:
           Women's First Round—Match #2—Heather
           Stupp vs. Karin Walton-Trent
01:00 PM   International Track & Field: Ivo Van Damme
           Meet from Brussels, Belgium
03:30 PM   Horseshow Jumping: The Cleveland Grand Prix
05:30 PM   ESPN's SportsWoman
06:00 PM   Unlimited Hydroplane Racing: The Columbia Cup
07:00 PM   ESPN NFL Football Special: 1982 NFC Preview
07:30 PM   SportsCenter
08:00 PM   ESPN's SportsForum—Wednesday Edition
08:30 PM   Auto Racing '82: NHRA Drag Racing North
           Star Nationals from Brainerd, MN
10:00 PM   Best of Notre Dame Football: 1979 Fighting
           Irish vs. Michigan
11:00 PM   SportsCenter

September 9, 1982

12:00 AM   CFL Football: Edmonton @ Calgary
02:30 AM   SportsCenter
03:30 AM   Auto Racing '82: NHRA Drag Racing North
           Star Nationals Show #2
05:00 AM   Exhibition Basketball: NBA All-Stars vs. Chinese
           Army Team from Shanghai, China
07:00 AM   SportsCenter

09:00 AM   ESPN's SportsWoman
09:30 AM   ESPN's SportsForum
10:00 AM   SportsCenter
12:00 AM   Auto Racing '82: CART AirCal 500 (3 hour
           version)
03:00 PM   ESPN Presents Saturday Night at the Fights:
           Main Event—Roberto Duran vs. Kirland Laing
05:30 PM   ESPN NFL Football Special: 1982 NFC Preview
06:00 PM   ESPN's SportsForum—Thursday Edition
06:30 PM   CFL Football: From the 55-Yard Line
07:00 PM   ESPN NFL Football Special: 1982 AFC Preview
07:30 PM   SportsCenter
08:00 PM   The NFL Story: Line by Line—Season Premiere
08:30 PM   Top Rank Boxing From Ft. Worth, TX
11:00 PM   SportsCenter

September 10, 1982

12:00 AM   Exhibition Basketball: NBA All-Stars vs. Chinese
           Army Team From Shanghai, China
02:00 AM   ESPN NFL Football Special: 1982 AFC Preview
02:30 AM   SportsCenter
03:30 AM   Top Rank Boxing From Ft. Worth, TX
06:00 AM   The NFL Story: Line by Line
06:30 AM   ESPN's SportsForum
07:00 AM   SportsCenter
09:00 AM   CFL Football: From the 55-Yard Line
09:30 AM   The NFL Story: Line by Line
10:00 AM   SportsCenter
12:00 PM   Top Rank Boxing From Ft. Worth, TX
02:30 PM   The NFL Story: Line by Line
03:00 PM   Auto Racing '82: NHRA Drag Racing North
           Star Nationals Show
04:30 PM   CFL Football: From the 55-Yard Line
05:00 PM   Exhibition Basketball #3: NBA All-Stars vs.
           Chinese Army Team from Shanghai, China
07:00 PM   Owens-Corning College Football Preview with
           Jim Simpson and Bud Wilkinson
07:30 PM   SportsCenter
08:00 PM   CFL Football: Hamilton @ Toronto

11:00 PM   SportsCenter

September 11, 1982

12:00 AM   Top Rank Boxing From Ft. Worth, TX
02:30 AM   SportsCenter
03:30 AM   Owens-Corning College Football Preview with
            Jim Simpson and Bud Wilkinson
04:00 AM   CFL Football: Hamilton @ Toronto
06:30 AM   ESPN's Sports Forum
07:00 AM   SportsCenter
08:00 AM   Best of Notre Dame Football: 1979 Fighting
            Irish vs. Michigan
09:00 AM   ESPN NFL Football Special: 1982 NFC Preview
09:30 AM   ESPN NFL Football Special: 1982 AFC Preview
10:00 AM   SportsCenter
11:00 AM   Owens-Corning College Football Preview with
            Jim Simpson and Bud Wilkinson
11:30 AM   NCAA Instructional Series #10 & #12: Soccer-
            Shooting and Volleyball-Passing, Setting and
            Spiking
12:00 PM   SportsCenter Plus
12:30 PM   NFL Game Of The Week—Season Preview
*1:00 PM   CFL Football: Hamilton @ Toronto
04:00 PM   Auto Racing '82: Austrian Grand Prix
*5:00 PM   PKA Full Contact Karate from Ft. Lauderdale, FL
            (time period extended to accommodate
            SportsCenter Plus)
07:00 PM   NFL Game Of The Week—Season Preview
07:30 PM   SportsCenter
08:30 PM   ESPN Presents Saturday Night at the Fights:
            Main Event—Gerrie Coetzee vs. Stan Ward
11:00 PM   SportsCenter

September 12, 1982

12:00 AM   CFL Football: Calgary @ Winnipeg
03:00 AM   SportsCenter

---

* SportsCenter Plus will present the latest news and scores
from the world of sports throughout the day, beginning at
noon Saturday and Sunday. The listed times of some
programs may be changed slightly.

04:00 AM	ESPN Presents Saturday Night at the Fights: Main Event—Gerrie Coetzee vs. Stan Ward
06:30 AM	Australian Rules Football: North melbourne vs. Essendon (R#1)
08:00 AM	SportsCenter
09:00 AM	College Football: Tulsa @ Arkansas
12:00 PM	SportsCenter Plus
12:30 PM	International Racquetball Championships #6: Men's Quarterfinal—Match #1—Marty Hogan vs. Bem Koltum
01:00 PM	Auto Racing '82: NASCAR Wrangler 400 from Richmond, VA
04:30 PM	Australian Rules Football: Richmond vs. Hawthorn
06:30 PM	"Down The Stretch": ESPN's Horse Racing Weekly
07:00 PM	SportsCenter
08:00 PM	College Football: West Virginia @ Oklahoma
11:00 PM	SportsCenter

Made in the USA
Monee, IL
19 November 2022